The Abortion Debate

ISSUES FOR THE NINETIES

Volume 34

Editor

Craig Donnellan

First published by Independence
PO Box 295
Cambridge CB1 3XP

British Library Cataloguing in Publication Data
The Abortion Debate – (Issues for the Nineties Series)
I. Donnellan, Craig II. Series
363.4'6

ISBN 1 86168 035 X

Printed in Great Britain
City Print Ltd,
Milton Keynes

Typeset by
Claire Boyd

Cover
The illustration on the front cover is by
Michaela Bloomfield.

CONTENTS

Chapter One: An overview

Chapter Two: The moral dilemma

Introduction

The Abortion Debate is the thirty-fourth volume in the series: **Issues For The Nineties**. The aim of this series is to offer up-to-date information about important issues in our world.

The Abortion Debate looks at ethical, legal and medical aspects of abortion.

The information comes from a wide variety of sources and includes:
Government reports and statistics
Newspaper reports and features
Magazine articles and surveys
Literature from lobby groups
and charitable organisations.

It is hoped that, as you read about the many aspects of the issues explored in this book, you will critically evaluate the information presented. It is important that you decide whether you are being presented with facts or opinions. Does the writer give a biased or an unbiased report? If an opinion is being expressed, do you agree with the writer?

The Abortion Debate offers a useful starting-point for those who need convenient access to information about the many issues involved. However, it is only a starting-point. At the back of the book is a list of organisations which you may want to contact for further information.

*****

CHAPTER ONE: AN OVERVIEW

Abortion key facts

Information from Marie Stopes International

Abortion is allowed for these reasons

A Risk of life to woman

B To prevent grave permanent injury to physical or mental health of woman

C Risk of injury to the physical or mental health of pregnant woman (up to 24 weeks)

D risk of injury to the physical or mental health of existing children (up to 24 weeks)

E Substantial risk of child being born seriously handicapped

When do most abortions take place?

Abortion was legalised in 1967 in the UK and is allowed up to 24 weeks, but could happen later in rare cases, such as to save the woman's life.

In 1995, 89% of abortions were carried out before the twelth week of pregnancy.

How many?

163,621 abortions were carried out in England and Wales in 1994. 9,323 of those women came from overseas, or from elsewhere in the British Isles, such as the Irish Republic, or Northern Ireland, where abortion is illegal.

Who has an abortion?

Women of all ages, religions and cultures have abortions. Some have no children, others already have families.

Most were using family planning but maybe had an accident with their contraceptive method or didn't use it properly.

Women have abortions for all sorts of reasons.
These include:

- having financial problems
- being single and lacking support
- being homeless
- having a family already
- not wanting children at all
- being pregnant as a result of incest or rape
- having relationship problems
- having a pregnancy which will result in a seriously handicapped baby

In 1994 abortion was most common in the 20-24 year age-group, which made up 26% (43,386) of all abortions.

How is abortion done?

Most abortions (those up to 12 weeks) are carried out by removing the contents of the uterus by gentle suction. This can be done under local or general anaesthetic and takes about 10 minutes. Later abortions involve gently opening the neck of the uterus (cervix) and removing the contents with an instrument.

Women who are less than nine weeks pregnant can choose the abortion pill (RU486). This causes them to have a miscarriage, but can take about six hours.

What does it cost?

In the UK, about half of all abortions are carried out on the National Health Service (NHS), which involves no cost. But a lot of women cannot get an NHS abortion because their health authority does not provide them, or because the waiting lists are too long. They may come to a charity such as Marie Stopes, where an abortion costs between £305 and £555, depending on how many weeks pregnant the woman is.

Who approves an abortion?

A women has to see two doctors to get permission, to check she understands her decision and is eligible. She does not have to see her own GP if she doesn't want him or her to know. She does not have to tell anyone except the clinic staff. If you are under 16 you should have the permission of a parent or guardian, but if this is not possible, a doctor can sometimes take responsibility.

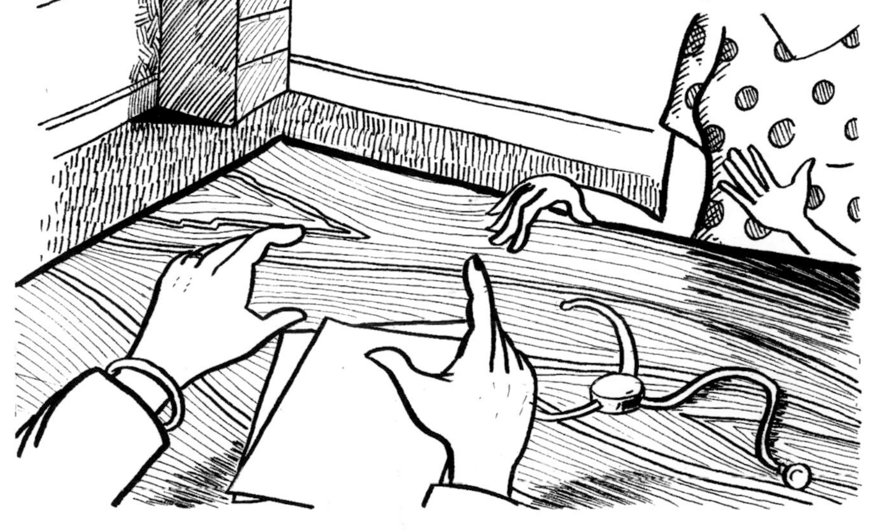

Abortion law

Information from British Pregnancy Advisory Service (BPAS)

The development of abortion law

Prior to 1803 English common law permitted abortion provided it was carried out before 'quickening', the point reached at about 20 – 24 weeks when it was believed the soul entered the body. Abortions performed after quickening were an offence under British common law, but there were no fixed penalties and the woman having the abortion was not necessarily held responsible. After 1803 the laws pertaining to abortion radically altered and termination became a criminal offence from the time of conception.

'In 1938, a Dr Alex Bourne performed an abortion on a 14-year-old girl after she had been raped by several soldiers. Dr Bourne later gave himself up to police. In court the judge ruled that Dr Bourne had acted in the "honest belief" that what he had done was to try to "preserve the life of the mother". This opened the way for a limited number of legal abortions to be carried out.'

'In 1991 a public opinion poll on the issue of abortion showed that 81% of women were in favour of personal choice. This was as high as 90% between the ages of 18 and 24.'

Abortion facts & figures by Leonora Lloyd, NAC education

The Offences Against the Person Act 1861

In 1861 Parliament passed the Offences Against the Persons Act. The 1861 Act Section 58 made abortion a criminal offence, punishable by imprisonment from three years to life even when performed for medical reasons. No further legal changes occurred in England until 1929. The two following laws provide the exceptions to this 1861 Act.

The Infant Life Preservation Act 1929

In 1929 the Infant Life Preservation Act amended the law stating it would no longer be regarded as a felony if abortion was carried out in good faith for the sole purpose of preserving the life of the mother. The Act made it illegal to kill a child 'capable of being born live', and enshrines 28 weeks as the age at which a foetus must be presumed to be viable. Importantly the Act vested doctors with the power to decide when abortion is legal in certain cases when the life of the mother is threatened. (NB. It is a criminal offence to abort a viable foetus of whatever age.)

In 1936 the Abortion Law Reform Association was formed as a consequence of feeling that abortion legislation in its present state was unsatisfactory. The Abortion Law Reform Association recommended that the law should be made clear, as the 1861 Act still on the statute books deemed abortion illegal under all circumstances, while the 1929 Act stated that abortion was legal when it was performed by a medical practitioner who was 'satisfied that the continuance of the pregnancy was liable to endanger the health of the expectant mother'.

By 1966 public opinion relating to abortion gathered momentum as it was felt by many people that there was a need for clarification and reform on abortion law. It was the feeling of society that legalising the operation for medical professionals was the only way in which the tragic social problems of illegal abortions could be prevented.

The Abortion Act 1967

The Abortion Act 1967 came into effect on 27 April 1968 and permits termination of pregnancy by a registered practitioner subject to certain conditions. Regulations under the Act mean that abortions must be performed by a registered medical practitioner in a National Health Service Hospital or in a Department of Health approved location – such as British Pregnancy Advisory Service Clinics. An abortion may be approved for the following reasons:

A The continuance of the pregnancy would involve risk to the life of the pregnant woman greater than if the pregnancy were terminated.

B The termination is necessary to prevent grave permanent injury to the physical or mental health of the pregnant woman.

C The continuance of the pregnancy would involve risk, greater than if the pregnancy were terminated, of injury to the physical or mental health of the pregnant woman.

D The continuance of the pregnancy would involve risk, greater than if the pregnancy were terminated, of injury to the physical or mental health of any existing child(ren) of the family of the pregnant woman.

E There is a substantial risk that if the child were born it would suffer from physical or mental abnormalities as to be seriously handicapped, or in emergency, certified by the operating practitioners as immediately necessary.

F To save the life of the pregnant woman; or

G To prevent grave permanent injury to the physical or mental health of the pregnant woman.

Later in 1990 amendments to the 1967 Abortion Act came into force through the Human Fertilisation & Embryology Act.

Human Fertilisation and Embryology Act 1990 (HFEA)

Section 37 of the HFEA later made the changes to the 1967 Abortion Act in making the time limit of abortion 24 weeks under statutory grounds C and D. Statutory grounds A, B and E are now without time limit.

Recent developments

In May 1996 the Termination of Pregnancy Restriction Bill was given its first reading in the House of Lords. The Bill, if passed, would amend the Abortion Act of 1967 so that to perform terminations on the sole ground of a diagnosis of Down's Syndrome would become illegal. The Bill was introduced into the House of Lords by the Conservative peer Viscount Brentford.

Although inconsistent and contradictory in its early legal development, the introduction of the Abortion Act of 1967 clarified the position on abortion and to this day provides the prominent statutory framework on which abortion is based.

NB. The Infant Life Preservation Act of 1929 does not apply to Scotland and the Abortion Act does not apply in Northern Ireland.

'3500 BC is the earliest recorded reference to the enactment of abortion.'

• The above is an extract from *Student Information*, published by BPAS British Pregnancy Advisory Service. See page 39 for address details.

The arguments for and against abortion

The arguments against abortion

- State that human life begins at conception and believe that abortion destroys respect for human life.
- Abortion is violent for the mother and child and is uncivilised and unjust.
- Abortion is unnecessary and alternatives can be found.
- Women suffer from Post Abortion Trauma which results in depression, guilt, broken relationships and emotional difficulties.
- Medical knowledge and science have advanced in recent years to such a degree that abortion is rarely necessary to save the life of the mother.
- Many women use abortion as a contraceptive method.
- Tests can show if a child in the womb is disabled – anti-abortion organisations often believe that the child needs help with the difficulties or disabilities it may be born with.
- Whenever and however abortions are performed, they always end up in the loss of at least one life, possibly two (not very often).

The arguments for abortion

- The fertilised egg is potential life, based on scientific evidence the foetus is not viable (capable of independent life) in the early stage of pregnancy and is still part of the mother.
- Abortion has existed throughout history and making it legally or socially unacceptable does not drive it away.
- If women are to lead healthy, happy lives and offer the same to any children they may have, they need to be able to exercise control over their reproductive lives.
- Making abortion illegal in the nineteenth century in the UK led women with unwanted pregnancies to try dangerous methods to induce abortion.
- Legal abortion is safe, particularly when it is carried out in the first 12 weeks of pregnancy.
- The lack of a 100% reliable form of contraceptive means that unplanned pregnancy is a reality even in countries where contraception is available.

'A 1995 MORI poll found that 66% of people questioned agreed that abortion should be "available on request" while only 15% strongly disagreed with this.'

The information contained within this article is presented in good faith and to the best ability of BPAS at the time of production. Sources of reference for certain content/statements includes: National Abortion Campaign Education Material; Education for Choice; Family Planning Association; BPAS Views

• The above is an extract from *Student Information*, published by BPAS British Pregnancy Advisory Service. See page 39 for address details.

Abortion

An introduction to the facts about abortion

Is it easy for a woman to get an abortion?
This depends chiefly on her reasons for wanting an abortion, how far pregnant she is, where she lives and sometimes her financial situation. Abortion up to about 12 weeks of pregnancy is a relatively simple operation. After this, it becomes increasingly complicated and may be riskier to the woman, so doctors may be less willing to carry out an abortion.

The abortion law is quite simple but it is the doctors who decide whether a woman qualifies for an abortion. Some doctors disagree with abortions and so will not co-operate in helping a woman to obtain one. Many doctors feel that if a woman really has made up her mind that she wants an abortion, then the risks to her mental and physical health will always be greater if she continues the unwanted pregnancy. These doctors will then generally support a woman's decision to have an abortion.

If consultant gynaecologists (medical specialists in women's health) at the local hospital are not very willing to do abortions it can be difficult for a woman living in that area to get an NHS abortion. Even then she may sometimes be able to get an abortion that is paid for by the NHS at a private clinic through an 'extra contractual referral' that is arranged by the clinic with the NHS but often she will have to pay the fees herself. Some women may have a struggle to find the money although some of the charitable agencies will arrange payment over a period of time. Otherwise such women have difficulty in getting an abortion.

Why do some people disagree with abortion?
Disagreement with abortion may

stem from a variety of views people hold, such as:

- the belief, based on religious or other views, that abortion, however early, involves taking a life because a new human being exists from the moment of conception
- the feeling that the availability of abortion implies a lowered respect for human life
- the anxiety that if a woman has an abortion, it may make it harder for her to conceive and to have a normal pregnancy when she wants one
- the worry that having an abortion may have a bad effect on a woman's mental health in the future
- the fear that if abortion is available people will become lazy about using efficient contraception (birth control)
- the concern that abortion reduces the number of babies available for adoption by childless couples.

Why do others agree with abortion?
Their agreement that abortion should be available is based on another set of views, such as:

- the belief that a new person does not exist until the foetus is born and capable of surviving independently of its mother's body
- the conviction that a woman should be allowed to choose whether or not she continues with her pregnancy, particularly since early abortion involves less risk to her physical and mental health than the later stages of pregnancy and childbirth
- the concern that every child should be wanted by his/her parents
- the feeling that a woman should not be asked to continue with her pregnancy only to give the baby away to another couple
- the belief that in some cases the health and well-being of the woman and her family may be placed at risk if she is forced to continue with the pregnancy
- the necessity for abortion to be available for special cases such as pregnancy due to rape, or incest, or a pregnancy in a very young girl or a much older woman, when it could have more than average risk
- when it is known that a pregnancy will very probably result in the birth of a seriously handicapped child.

How does a woman know she's pregnant?
The usual first sign of pregnancy is a missed period. Some women may also feel sick (often called 'morning sickness'), have tender breasts and have to pass urine more frequently than usual. There may be other causes for all these things, but if a woman has reason to think she might be pregnant, because she has had sexual intercourse with or without contraception, then she should find out for certain. This should be done without delay particularly if she thinks she might want an abortion – waiting will make her worry, perhaps without cause. If she is pregnant, by the time she knows for certain from other signs, her pregnancy will be more advanced and that could make an abortion more complicated.

Can a woman prevent a pregnancy if she knows she has had sexual intercourse without a reliable form of contraception?

If she acts quickly and visits a doctor, a family planning clinic or a Brook Advisory Centre within 72 hours (i.e. three days) of having sexual intercourse without a reliable form of contraception, she can be given emergency contraception (a special dose of hormonal pills). Up to 5 days after unprotected sexual intercourse, an IUD (which used to be called 'the coil') can be fitted to prevent a pregnancy. Also, some casualty departments can prescribe emergency contraception. Some doctors who disagree with abortion also disagree with emergency contraception and may not prescribe it. Emergency contraception usually prevents a pregnancy starting, but fails to do this for about 1 woman in 50 who use it.

How does she find out for certain that she is pregnant?

When a woman's period is a day or so overdue, a specimen of her urine can be tested for signs of pregnancy. Pregnancy tests can be arranged, often without charge, by a family doctor, or done by some family planning clinics, a Brook Advisory Centre, a Pregnancy Advisory Centre or some pharmacists. Women's groups often do free testing. Reliable do-it-yourself kits can be bought in pharmacies but cost from £8-£12.

If the test result is positive it is most likely that she is pregnant. If the test result is negative, she may be asked to return for a second test as it might be too soon for the pregnancy to affect her urine.

After about 16 weeks of pregnancy, some types of urine tests are not reliable, but a doctor would be able to examine the woman and from the size of her uterus (womb) will know if she is pregnant and how far advanced her pregnancy is. Ultrasound scans can be used when necessary to confirm pregnancy and to give more accurate information about the age of the foetus.

What are the reasons a woman might give for wanting an abortion?

She might want an abortion for medical reasons, such as:

- there is an illness in her family, or the father's family, that the baby could inherit
- she had a rubella infection early in her pregnancy so is afraid the baby might be handicapped
- she took drugs or medicine during her pregnancy that could have affected the development of the foetus
- she is suffering from mental or physical illness that might be worsened by pregnancy and childbirth.

She might want an abortion for other reasons, such as:

- she feels she just could not cope with a baby and her health would be likely to suffer
- the pregnancy was forced on her because she was raped
- she is an older woman and her family has grown up and because of her age there is an increased risk of having a handicapped baby
- her family will suffer if she has another child
- she did not understand the need for contraception to prevent pregnancy
- she is under 16 so is unable to be financially independent of her parents or to marry
- her boyfriend has left her and if she had a baby she would lose her job and her accommodation
- she definitely did not want to get pregnant but her method of contraception failed.

Some women may have many reasons for wanting an abortion while others may only have one.

• The above is an extract from *Abortion – An introduction to the facts about abortion*, produced by Brook Advisory Centres. See page 39 for address details.

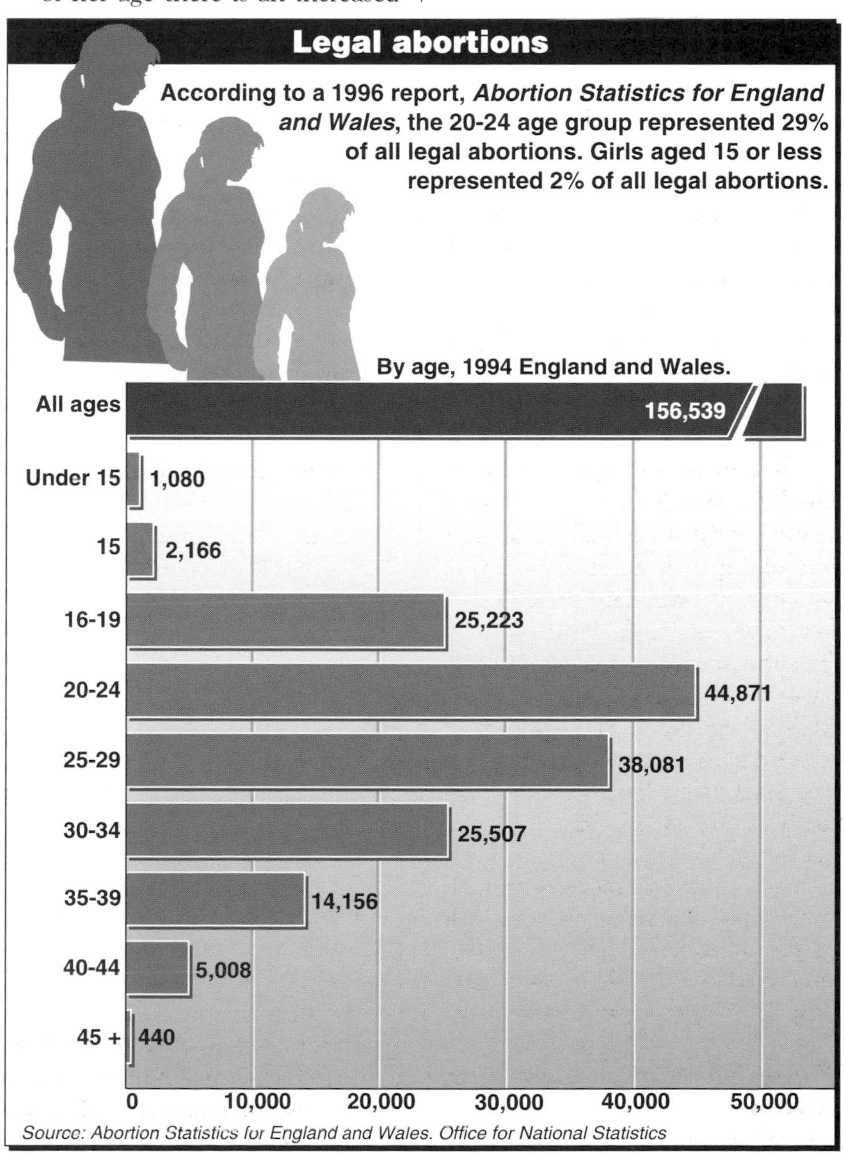

A matter of life or death

Who's who in the abortion debate

By Catherine Elsworth

Pro-life groups

Pro-Life Alliance: political party fielding 50 candidates in the general election; campaigning to outlaw 'any destruction of human life even at its most embryonic stage'. Believes abortion to be most important political issue.

Society for the Protection of Unborn Children (SPUC): set up to oppose the 1967 Abortion Act; aims to outlaw abortion, or, in its words, restore legal protection of unborn children. Main work: lobbying, education and campaigning.

British Victims of Abortion: group for and run by women who have had abortions; committed to 'exposing the truth of abortion's tragedy . . . and securing greater understanding of Post-Abortion Syndrome'. A subsidiary of SPUC.

LIFE: charity established in 1970, aims to relieve poverty and distress suffered by women before, during and after pregnancy; provides practical assistance and counselling.

Humanae Vitae House: Catholic pro-life movement; aims to persuade people to oppose abortion. Campaigners attend the 'abortion centres where they kill the babies' to stage sit-ins, pray for and counsel women.

Pro-Life Action Network: works closely with the spiritual pro-life movement; provides much of the support of and care for women who decide not to have an abortion.

Family and Youth Concern: group concerned with 'respecting life from the moment of conception until natural death'. Runs education programmes.

Comment on Reproductive Ethics: deals with bio-ethical questions surrounding reproductive issues, such as cloning, abortion and practices involving the 'destruction' of human life.

Pro-abortion groups

Pro-Choice Alliance: loose umbrella group comprising political and pro-abortion groups.

The Abortion Law Reform Association: pressure group behind the 1967 Abortion Act. Wants the law changed to ensure abortion is available free, on demand.

Brook Advisory Centres: professional youth-centred organisation providing contraceptive advice and counselling. Conducts pregnancy tests and referrals for abortion.

Birth Control Trust: charity providing information on issues surrounding sexual and reproductive health, including abortion; proposes ways in which health authorities and others can make services 'as women-friendly as possible'.

National Abortion Campaign: set up in 1973 to protect the 1967 Abortion Act. Now campaigning to extend it to make abortion available 'on request'.

British Pregnancy Advisory Service: largest provider of treatment for unplanned pregnancies outside NHS. Services include abortion, contraception, sterilisation. A non-profit-making charity.

Education for Choice: provides information on legal and ethical issues surrounding abortion.

Post-Abortion Counselling: counsels women after an abortion. Helps them take responsibility for their decision and deal with problems that have arisen, such as feelings of guilt.

Family Planning Association: charity providing sexual health and family planning advice; gives information on where to get help for either abortions or support for keeping the baby.

Religious views on abortion

Most religious leaders have put forward their views on abortion at some time, but even where they have been strongly against abortion, this does not seem to have had much effect on the behaviour of the women who follow that religion – every society seems to have abortion and some Roman Catholic countries, for example, have very high rates of (illegal) abortion.

Christian Religions

Roman Catholic Church

The Pope has never proclaimed an infallible teaching on abortion, although the Pope and most bishops believe it is morally wrong. There is also no Church teaching about when ensoulment and personhood occur. The Church does teach that the conscience of a person is the final guide to action.

In practice, the Catholic Church is officially against abortion and in countries where it is the dominant religion it has held out against abortion being legalised, not always successfully – e.g. France, Italy and Spain.

The official Canon Law of the Church states that anyone who commits the sin of abortion automatically excommunicates herself from the Church. This means that the person who decides to have an abortion has to think that her particular abortion, taking into account all the circumstances of her life and pregnancy, is a sin against God, and yet still decide to go ahead. If she does not believe it is a sin against God, because of her circumstances, it does not need to be confessed and is not a sin.

The official Church is also opposed to contraception and the current Pope has stated that all acts of sex must be 'open to conception' and this has been understood to mean that even the use of the 'safe period' is not allowed, and that indeed the only purpose of sexual intercourse is to conceive a child.

Protestants

Different Protestant groups hold different positions, but most stress the rights of individual conscience before God. They also rely on the Bible for guidance, but only one passage in the Bible refers – remotely – to the subject of abortion: Exodus 21:22. This states that if two men are fighting and wound a pregnant women, they shall have to pay her husband a fine if she has a miscarriage, but they will have to give a life for a life if the woman herself dies. The difference in punishments indicates that early biblical writers did not consider that the woman and the foetus had equal status – the foetus was not considered a person.

Early Protestant Reformers had an even stricter view of abortion than the Catholic Church of the time, partly based on their strict views about sex and marriage, the prime purpose of which they considered was procreation. Some Protestant sects still hold this view. But the majority no longer do so and much wider views on abortion prevail. Protestantism believes in freedom of conscience without coercion from secular or religious authorities. Many Protestant churches, therefore, have an official position of liberalism on the subject of abortion, although as this is a continuing debate the position is constantly shifting slightly.

Orthodox

This branch of Christianity covers mainly Greece, Russia and Eastern European countries. It teaches that the taking and administration of drugs for the purpose of causing abortion is wrong, but does not specifically outlaw other methods of abortion, which might indicate that it was the health of the woman that was of concern, as in the past drugs used to procure an abortion would be more likely to harm the woman than work as she hoped.

Judaism

Judaism has traditionally taught a respect for life, including pre-natal life, and in Jewish law there is an absolute right to life – but no absolute right to be born. An unborn life is not considered to be a person and does not become so until the head or the greater part has been born, after which it cannot be killed even to save the life of the mother. In fact, abortion when needed to save the life of the mother was required in Jewish law, and rabbinic teaching is still that the mother's welfare is the most important consideration. The traditional teaching, therefore, is that abortion of a defective foetus to save it pain is not permitted, but it is allowed to save the mother the psychological pain of bearing such a child.

Jews have a positive duty to procreate, which leads some Jews to see abortion, not as murder, but as immoral. In practice, Orthodox and conservative Jews are generally more anti-abortion than liberal and Reform Jews.

Other religions

Confucius taught that it was important to have sons, an attitude that still affects Chinese and Japanese society today, but both these nations use abortion as an important form of birth control.

Hinduism has a doctrine of non-interference with natural processes and so is against birth control and abortion, although one Hindu teacher taught that abortion was acceptable to save the life of the woman.

Buddhism, which started in India and spread to China and Japan, teaches the transmigration of souls, in which during successive lives the soul tries to reach Nirvana (like heaven). An abortion would interrupt this journey and thus is not permissible; in practice, abortion and infanticide were widely practised in Japan when Buddhism was the main religion.

Islam grew out of the teachings of Muhammad, who urged his followers to marry and procreate and allowed polygamy (more than one wife) so long as the man could support all his wives. There is no bar on birth control in Islamic writing. In practice, Islamic leaders have taken a conservative stance on abortion, and some still do so today – in Iran, a woman having an abortion faces the death penalty and woman's chief role is seen as producing sons. However, other Islamic leaders have declared that abortion is acceptable until the foetus achieves human form, put at 120 days.

Abortion statistics

How many women have abortions?

In 1995 there were 154,300 legally induced abortions to residents of England and Wales and 11,400 to residents of Scotland in 1994*.

When are abortions carried out?

In 1995 in England and Wales:

- 42% of abortions were carried out before the 9th week of pregnancy
- 47% of abortions were carried out between the 9th and 12th week of pregnancy
- 8% of abortions were carried out between the 13th and 16th week of pregnancy
- 2% of abortions were carried out between the 17th and 20th week of pregnancy
- Less than 1% of abortions were carried out at 20 weeks or later.

In Scotland in 1994, 61% of abortions were carried out before the 10th week of pregnancy, with 99.5% carried out before the 20th week.

NHS and non-NHS abortions

In 1995 in England and Wales, 70.5% of abortions to residents were paid for by the NHS. In 1994 in Scotland, 98% of abortions were paid for by the NHS.

Extremes in regional provision of NHS-funded abortions

In 1995 in the Northern and Yorks Region, 88% of all abortions were funded through the NHS, compared with only 61% in the North Thames Region. NHS provision by District Health Authority varied from 96% (Northumberland, Tees and Coventry) to 28% (North West Lancs).

Age of woman

1995 in England and Wales (Scottish figures in brackets)

- 2% (2%) of abortions were to women under 16
- 16% (20%) of abortions were to women aged 16-19
- 28% (31%) of abortions were to women aged 20-24
- 24% (21%) of abortions were to women aged 25-29
- 17% (14%) of abortions were to women aged 30-34
- 9% (8%) of abortions were to women aged 35-39
- 3% (3%) of abortions were to women aged 40-44
- Less than 0.5% of abortions were to women aged 45+

Married and single women

1995 in England and Wales (1994 Scottish figures in brackets)

- 66% (69%) of abortions were to single women
- 22% (21%) of abortions were to married women
- 8% (9%) of abortions were to divorced, separated or widowed women. (Remainder unstated.)

Risks to life

For the last ten years, approximately one woman a year has died as a result of legal abortion.

In 1994, in England and Wales, 50 women died from complications of pregnancy, childbirth and the puerperium.

Risks to mental health

A large review of studies into the long-term psychological effects of abortion found that the majority of women report positive reactions to the abortion with only a small minority expressing any long-lasting degree of regret. Negative feelings are most likely to be associated with abortion for foetal abnormality, later abortions, ambivalence about the decision and a history of psychiatric problems before the abortion. When women are refused abortions, up to 30% report negative feelings towards their child and difficulty adjusting.

Public opinion

Research in 1991 found that 81% of the adult population agreed that women should have the right to choose an abortion in the first three months of pregnancy.

References:
Office of Population Censuses & Surveys Monitor AB95/8.
Abortion Law Reform Association. *A Report on NHS Abortion Services*. 1997
The Psychological Sequelae of Therapeutic Abortion – Denied and Completed. P. Dagg, *Am. J. Psychiatry*, May 1991.
Series DH2 Mortality Statistics: Cause. OPCS
Harris Opinion Poll 1991.

* Latest available statistics

The campaign for choice

A more liberal abortion law

The Abortion Law Reform Association (ALRA) has been working since 1936 to enshrine in law and in practice a woman's right to safe, free and legal abortion based upon her own informed choice. The 1967 Abortion Act was a huge step forward but it does not go far enough.

Why do we want to change the abortion law?

It does not give women the right to choose

The power to decide whether a woman is entitled to abortion rests with her doctors. This cannot be right: nobody knows better than the woman herself when and if she is ready for motherhood. Doctors are burdened with a responsibility for which they are neither adequately trained nor necessarily suited.

The grounds for abortion are badly defined

Doctors have immense power of discretion when 'permitting' abortion: some of them interpret the law liberally, others very strictly. Not only is this unfair, it also leads to doctors abusing their power by indulging their personal options, even prejudices. Women feel humiliated and degraded by this process, and so do doctors.

It builds in delay

Everyone agrees that if abortion is to happen, it should take place as early in pregnancy as possible. By requiring two doctors to certify that a woman has legal grounds prior to termination, the law builds in delay.

It does not ensure adequate provision of abortion services

There is no statutory obligation for health authorities to provide abortion care to those who need it. Overall, about seven out of ten abortions are funded under the NHS, but this varies widely according to where you live and what priorities have been set by your health authority or trust.

It does not extend to Northern Ireland

Women in Northern Ireland are not entitled to the same treatment as those in the rest of the UK. Each year, many hundreds have to travel overseas to get the abortions they need.

What changes do we want?

ALRA is calling for a new abortion law, one which allows women the right to decide for themselves whether or not they are ready for motherhood, at least in the first three months of pregnancy. Instead of having to obtain the approval of two doctors they would see one doctor who would give them medical advice, information and access to counselling if they wanted it.

Doctors with a conscientious objection to abortion would still be allowed to opt out of abortion treatment, but they should be obliged to declare this objection, and to make clear a woman's right to see or be referred to another doctor.

As well as establishing women's right to choose, we want to guarantee their access to services to make that choice a reality. So we think health authorities should be obliged to provide comprehensive and easily available family planning, pregnancy testing, counselling and abortion services to meet the needs of local women. Hospitals should provide daycare services, where women could refer themselves without first being required to see their GP, and where abortions could be carried out separately from other gynaecological procedures.

Last but not least, we want women in Northern Ireland to be given abortion rights at least equivalent to those enjoyed on the mainland.

So if the law is changed . . .

. . . won't women be encouraged to use abortion instead of contraception?

No. Everybody agrees that prevention is better than cure, and ALRA would like to see the abortion rate reduced by better sex education and contraceptive use. We know that women find unplanned pregnancy and abortion a distressing experience, and there is no evidence that they risk it in preference to contraception.

. . . won't the number of abortions soar?

No. The abortion rate has come down in recent years. Those women who really want abortions get them – often by travelling great distances and at considerable expense to themselves. Abortion law reform will simply lessen the difficulties for those women.

. . . can the NHS afford to do all abortions?

Yes. The cost of early abortion is not great and would be further reduced by cutting bureaucracy and streamlining the procedure. In any case, women facing unplanned pregnancy are taxpayers also, and deserve good healthcare regardless of their ability to pay.

. . . how can you be sure women will make the right choice?

How can you be sure doctors make the right choice? There are no guarantees that women facing unplanned pregnancy won't later regret whatever decision they take, any more than we can guarantee that they will marry the right people or bring their children up well. But we can say with confidence that, provided they are given the right information and support to reach a fully informed choice, most women will know what is best for them and their loved ones.

. . . why should NHS staff be forced to participate in abortions they don't agree with?

The law protects the rights of health workers with a genuine conscientious objection to abortion. We would agree that it is better for women seeking abortions to be treated by staff who are sympathetic to their situation. However, we don't think doctors and nurses should be able to pick and choose to be involved with some abortions and not others – any more than they can pick and choose between patients in other areas of healthcare. To give women the right to choose on abortion, both in law and in practice, ALRA proposes the following five changes to the 1967 Abortion Act:

1 abortion on request in the first three months of pregnancy
2 and then only one doctor's approval up to 24 weeks
3 a duty on doctors to declare their conscientious objection
4 inclusion of Northern Ireland
5 a duty on the NHS to provide abortion services

Abortion

The British Humanist Association's view

Humanists are guided by reason and compassion, rather than dogmatic rules. They have positive moral values and use these to make decisions on ethical questions.

Humanists think that there is no absolute 'for' or 'against' rule on abortion. The practical aspects of each case must be considered. Decision should not be made according to a fixed cultural ideology.

Humanists respect life and are concerned for the quality of each life. They think it is better to prevent an unwanted pregnancy rather than terminate it once it has occurred.

Not all humanists agree on all the medical, legal and ethical issues raised when discussing cases of abortion. However they do try to discuss them rationally, looking at each problem as a whole and examining every aspect of it.

No single decision can be applied in all cases.

In England, Scotland and Wales an abortion may be legally performed before the twenty-fourth week of pregnancy if two doctors agree that:

1 There will be a greater risk to the life of the mother if the pregnancy continues
2 There will be a greater risk to the health, mental or physical, of the mother if the pregnancy continues
3 There will be a greater risk to the health, mental or physical, of the children of the family if the pregnancy continues
4 There is a substantial risk that the baby will be born handicapped

After twenty-four weeks of pregnancy the foetus is considered viable, although such a baby will need many weeks of care in a premature baby unit, and is not guaranteed survival.

Today there are very few maternal illnesses for which doctors would unequivocally recommend a termination of pregnancy.

Most terminations are performed under category 2, or categories 2 and 3 together. These are usually unplanned and are often the first or last pregnancy of the woman.

In general the decision to seek a termination of an unwanted pregnancy is taken by the couple responsible but humanists believe that the woman should have the right to choose a termination herself if she wishes it after counselling.

A few planned pregnancies do not develop perfectly.

Some abnormalities are discovered which are incompatible with life after delivery. Few parents or doctors would wish such a pregnancy to continue to term.

Other abnormalities are discovered which are known to lead to disability and a higher level of dependency on others. Some parents feel that they can cope with this. Others cannot. Some do not wish to force their child to live such a life.

In these last cases all possible information must be given to the prospective parents so that they can come to a joint decision with their medical advisers.

Having thought about many different situations, and the implications of abortion for the mother, the embryo or foetus, and other people concerned, humanists generally share these views:

- abortion can be the morally right option in many circumstances
- the human foetus does not gain the status of a human person until some time into its development
- women should have control over their own bodies
- society should provide safe, legal abortion facilities
- improved sex education would reduce the number of abortions
- because some people are opposed to abortion does not mean that they should be able to take the choice away from other people
- society should not force women to have unwanted children
- obstacles should not be placed in front of women wanting an abortion so that it has to take place unnecessarily late.

If you would like a full publications list or information on a specific topic, please write to: BHA, 47 Theobalds Road, London WC1X 8SP. Or you can call us on (0171) 430 0908.

We welcome your comments too.

Growing support for abortion

Two-thirds of adults would grant it on demand, says poll

By Sian Clare and Alastair Dalton

Abortion on demand is backed by two-thirds of the population of Britain, an increase of 10 per cent over the past 17 years, according to an opinion poll published yesterday.

The MORI survey found that 64 per cent of people agreed with the statement 'abortion should be made legally available for all who want it', compared with 54 per cent in 1980.

There was 95 per cent support for abortion where the woman's life was in danger, 91 per cent support where her health was at risk and 88 per cent support where she had been raped.

However, the poll showed a significant drop in the number of people backing abortion where it was likely the baby would be born mentally or physically handicapped – 67 and 66 per cent respectively, compared to 84 and 81 per cent in 1980. Where the pregnant woman was under 16, there was 58 per cent support for the right to an abortion (69 per cent), but where a woman's reason for a termination was financial, 51 per cent disapproved.

The poll, commissioned by the Birth Control Trust, which supports the right of women to make their own choices about abortion, was described as the most definitive study of public attitudes to abortion since 1980.

David Paintin, the trust's chairman, said the poll showed that although opponents of abortion were vocal they represented only a minority view.

'Politicians and policy makers need to be aware that the option of abortion is essential for women's health and well-being in many circumstances, and that there is support from a majority of the people in the country for this,' he said.

However, the Society for the Protection of Unborn Children, said that the survey results were 'highly inconsistent'. Its spokesman, Brendan Gerard, said: 'It is highly questionable to say that this poll demonstrates a shift towards support for abortion on demand.

'We have never denied that a majority of people support abortion in certain circumstances. The key issue is: do people support a situation where abortion is available virtually on demand? Survey results on those terms suggest not.' The poll findings come as abortion rises up the political agenda, with the Pro Life Alliance planning to field some 70 candidates at the general election, up to 15 of them in Scotland. Bruno Quintavalle, director of the alliance, which is planning to show an abortion in a party political broadcast during the election campaign, said: 'One thing that has not changed since 1980 is the widespread ignorance of what abortion involves.' The poll showed that 50 per cent of Roman Catholics backed the right to an abortion – contravening the Church's teaching – while 38 per cent disagreed.

The pollsters attempted to explain the apparent conflict between the proportion of respondents backing the legal right to an abortion 'for all who want it', yet not approving of abortion in certain circumstances. They suggested the figures showed a substantial number of adults thought abortion should be legal, even in circumstances where they personally did not approve of it.

The poll involved 1,943 people throughout Britain aged 15 or above between 7 and 11 February.

*A recent BBC Frontline Scotland poll which showed most Catholics were in favour of abortion has been attacked in *Flourish*, the Glasgow Archdiocese newspaper.

The newspaper said that the Catholic Church's criticism of the poll was backed by Gordon Heald, former managing director of polling company Gallup, who said the way the questions were put biased the outcome.

Abortion – the key issue

Information from the Christian Medical Fellowship

The key issue in the abortion debate, is 'What constitutes a human being?' as Scripture clearly forbids the killing of innocent human beings.[1] When does a zygote or embryo become a human being and therefore assume the right not to be killed?

One recent author has argued that this must be at the point that the 'spirit' enters the body and from Old Testament references[2] has suggested that this must take place before birth. He then postulates six weeks as the time on the basis of the fact that the first blood cells are formed at this time, and that the Bible states that the life is in the blood.[3]

When does life really begin?

Different translation points have been suggested by other authors. The more popular ones have been implantation (one week), neural crest stage (14 days), rudimentary circulation (21 days), breathing movements (12 wks), viability (approx 24 wks) and birth. The problem with most of these is that they are either difficult to define exactly in time, or occur at variable stages in gestation. As a result they may not give us a cut-off mark which is of any practical use in making decisions. For example, neural crest development, blood formation and circulation and breathing movements develop over a period of time. At what point in a continuous process do we draw the line? Viability is dependent on a multiplicity of factors including maturity at a given gestation, pharmacological intervention and the level of neonatal intensive care available. To take birth as the divider is ridiculous as Andrew points out. What qualitative difference is there between an infant one minute before and one minute

after birth? Furthermore are we to say that a premature infant at 25 weeks gestation on a ventilator is a human being while a post-term infant of 42 weeks still *in utero* is not?

Where do we draw the line?

Human development is a continuous process beginning with fertilisation. Essentially the only difference between a fertilised ovum and a full-term baby is nutrition and time. The genetic code is present in full from the very beginning. A fertilised ovum is human certainly. It is not a cat or a snake or a cabbage – and certainly it is alive! It possesses at least in rudimentary form those attributes of a living thing – movement, respiration, sensitivity, growth, reproduction, excretion and nutrition. By virtue of being alive is it not then a 'being'? And by virtue of being a human is it not then a 'human being'? Not a 'potential' human being but rather a human being with potential, a potential foetus, infant or adult. Should it not then be accorded the rights that any human being has by virtue of being made in the image of God?[4] At least at zygote or embryo stage it has not yet committed any capital offence.

What about the spirit?

But I hear you saying, 'this is all very well but when does the spirit enter? – it is that which we do not know for sure and it is that which determines when a fertilised ovum becomes a human being with rights.' Is this a valid question? Some Christians have said that human beings cannot be divided into body and spirit at all, that this is an ancient Greek idea which finds no support

Scripture clearly forbids the killing a of human being

in the Bible. But is this really true? There must be something that survives death. What is it that is further clothed by a new resurrection body? What is it that faces judgement? What is the 'earthly tent' that Paul talks of? The Bible does support a spirit-body 'dualism' of some sort. So to ask when the spirit enters the body is a valid question. So when does it? We know from Scripture that God 'knows us' (which implies that we must be human beings in the sense of having rights) even 'before' he forms us[5] and we have argued before that the formation of a human being is a continuous process beginning at conception. Is it not then quite possible that the zygote is a human being from the moment of fertilisation? Or to put it another way – how can we be sure that the 'spirit' (if indeed it enters the developing human at all) does not enter at fertilisation? This seems a very logical time, being the point at which human life begins. If we can't be sure that the spirit doesn't enter at the time of fertilisation, then how can we be sure that by prescribing the 'morning after' pill or by inserting an intra-uterine 'contraceptive' device (IUCD) we are not taking the life of a human being? It seems we must admit that at lest there is a possibility that we are. Should we not then err on the side of caution?

But how can a zygote have a relationship with God?

But you object. How could a single-celled zygote which contains no differentiated neurological tissue and is not even aware of its own existence be in any sort of relationship with God? If it is incapable of any relationship then how can it possess any personal status? This sounds like a good argument. But doesn't it misunderstand the whole concept of being made in the image of God? The status of the embryo is derived not from the fact that it knows God in any sense. Clearly it is incapable of this. Its status is derived from the fact that God knows it. Its dignity does not depend on its own personal attributes but is rather given to it by God.

But doesn't God himself terminate embryos?

Another argument for not regarding embryos as human beings is the fact that 40% to 70% of normal embryos are lost in their first month of life. This is a peculiar argument. One cannot argue that personal status is somehow dependent on likelihood of survival. We would not dare argue for instance that because infant mortality is high in developing countries as a result of adverse environmental conditions or poor nutrition we should therefore be justified in killing malnourished or deprived infants ourselves. Our usual response as doctors in this situation would be to find out why the mortality rate was so high and if possible to do something about it. If no intervention is practicable then we do not conclude that those who died were therefore not human beings. Nor can we argue that since God allows large numbers of embryos to die he himself therefore must not regard them as human beings. This is to put ourselves in the position of God and to presume that we know his purposes when he has not chosen to reveal them to us. Even if we are to say that God himself is the greatest terminator of embryos, this does not give us licence to join him in the destruction. God may give and take life as he chooses. It is his sovereign right as God. It is not our right. We may only exercise those rights which he specifically delegates to us and destroying embryos is not one of them.

What about the embryo who was God incarnate?

We might ask at what stage the 'spirit' of Christ entered the embryo of God incarnate. If Christ was indeed conceived by the power of the Holy Spirit would it not be reasonable to assume that the Holy Spirit entered at conception?

Conclusions

Although I cannot demonstrate with certainty that the human embryo possesses a 'spirit', I have demonstrated that there is good enough reason to believe that it may. It follows therefore that we should refrain from deliberately destroying it.

What is the point of all this argument? The point is that as doctors we are not merely armchair theorists. We must make moral decisions and carry them out in the real world. By our practice we will set an example to those who follow. For our practice we will be accountable to God.

For these reasons I am unable to accept the previous author's conclusions. If we hold that the embryo does not become a human being until 4 to 6 weeks gestation – then we can have no real objection to destruction of embryos *in vitro*, experimentation with embryos, freezing of embryos, selling of embryos for profit, cloning of embryos, genetic engineering or selective destruction of embryos on genetic grounds. Pandora's Box has opened too far. It is far better to suffer the consequences of not fitting IUCDs than to be party to the destruction of what may well be the most innocent and defenceless form of human life there is. Although only the blueprint for an erythrocyte resides in the developing embryo, it is enough.

References
1 Exodus 20:13; Deuteronomy 5:17; Leviticus 24:17-22
2 Isaiah 49:1,5; Jeremiah 1:5; Psalm 139:13-16
3 Genesis 9:4
4 Genesis 9:5,6; James 3:9; Colossians 3:10
5 Jeremiah 1:5

• The above is an extract from pages 24-28 of the April 1992 edition of *Nucleus*, the student journal of the Christian Medical Fellowship.

Would you take your daughter to the abortion clinic?

Should a mother encourage her teenage daughter to have an abortion?

It's probably the most heart-wrenching moment a parent can ever face. Your teenage daughter comes home and tells you she's pregnant. Do you encourage her to have an abortion? After all, a baby at her age will ruin her life. Or do you persuade her to go through with the pregnancy and keep the child? After all, the gift of life is a precious thing. According to latest statistics 165,000 women a year have an abortion. Here two mums reveal what they advised their daughters .

No, says Brenda Davies

Brenda, 46, of Belper, Derbyshire, was stunned when she found out that her 16-year-old daughter Katy had been made pregnant by a boy she met in a pub.

But she had a compelling way of persuading her daughter that continuing with the pregnancy was the only way ahead.

'I have seven daughters and one son and Katy is the third eldest. She was in her GCSE year at comprehensive school when it happened.

'I had a hunch something was up. Call it a mother's intuition. She was starting to act tetchy and become withdrawn.

'One day one of her teachers rang me and asked me to come into school. When I arrived she took me to one side, asked me to sit down and told me that she had just accompanied Katy to a clinic for a pregnancy test and that the result was positive.

'When Katy said she was pregnant, I surprised her and the teacher by telling them, "So am I". I had just found out and they were the first people I told.

'I immediately told Katy that having a baby would not be the end of her life – it would be the start of someone else's.

'It's a natural thing for unmarried girls who become pregnant to think that they have nothing to look forward to and for some of them to consider abortions.

'But they are wrong. It's something to celebrate. Both my baby and Katy's were due on the same day. But she had hers a week early – two weeks before mine, which was overdue.

'Having Paul didn't ruin Katy's education, as many parents fear.

'She got her GCSEs and A-levels – and finally a degree in psychology at university.

'Now Katy is studying for her Masters, and looking after Paul and her second child, Isaac, who she conceived during a brief fling with another man.

'Isaac comes to lectures with her. Katy even breast-feeds him in front of the other students.

'She's a wonderful mother and a great daughter.'

Yes, says Diane Roberts

Diane, 40, from Birmingham supported her 18-year-old daughter through the traumatic process of an abortion. Here she talks frankly about her decision.

'My daughter was at college and had been seeing someone for about 18 months.

'The first I knew she was pregnant was when I got a tearful phone call one night telling me what had happened. Her boyfriend didn't want to know. He dropped her immediately.

Your teenage daughter comes home and tells you she's pregnant. Do you encourage her to have an abortion?

'My daughter's father and I had divorced. So I became in effect the only person she had in the world. It was left to the two of us to make up our minds what to do.

'For the days and weeks we agonised about it, we went through the most terrible heartache I have ever known.

'Either way it is a decision without a happy outcome.

'Logically my daughter knew she couldn't go through with the pregnancy. It would have meant giving up her education, perhaps living on benefit, who knows what the result would have been. And all the while the time clock was ticking away. You only have a few weeks to decide what to do. In the end it came down to what my daughter wanted. And she wanted to have the termination.

'She went in for surgery eight weeks after becoming pregnant. It is supposed to be the best time – if you can call any time a good time

'The clinic was a big, rambling country house and the staff were very sympathetic.

'My daughter and I went together, of course. The waiting room was full of people.

'I sat with my daughter and held her hand, both before and after. I was even there when she was given her pre-med.

'She was only in the operating room for 15 minutes and we went home together that same day.

'When she came out of the operation, her feeling was one of intense relief.

'It was a saddening experience for both of us – but there were no regrets and there haven't been since. We both know we did the right thing.'

Three reasons why abortion is not the answer

Scotland's Catholic leader tells why he'll always fight for the right to life

By Cardinal Thomas Winning

I have sometimes wondered what I'd choose as my specialist subject in the unlikely event of being asked to appear on *Mastermind*.

And the answer I've come up with is not philosophy or theology or canon law, but 'people'.

If almost 50 years as a priest and 25 years as a bishop makes you an enthusiast for anything, it makes you an enthusiast for people.

I suppose it was that desire to serve people – my own people in Lanarkshire in the 1930s – that first made me think about becoming a priest.

And as a Cardinal, that love of people is still what motivates me to speak out on areas of basic human rights.

Over the years I've been critical of the abortion laws in this country. How can I be anything else? As a Catholic, indeed as a human being, I can't sit back and allow unborn babies to be killed just because their existence is inconvenient.

Yet that's the reality in Britain today.

There's a massive gulf between the reality of abortion virtually on demand and the tight constraints on abortion foreseen by those who drew up the law in the 1960s.

My convictions are only strengthened when I go round the parishes and meet people whose lives have been affected, one way or another, by the Abortion Act. People like Gerard Higgins.

Gerard's the head altar server at St Gabriel's Parish in Cathcart, Glasgow.

'Nowadays, abortion has replaced adoption as the logical conclusion of an unplanned pregnancy'

He's a big strong lad whom I've watched grow up over the years. In fact, recently he made me laugh when I visited the parish. He came in after Mass and said to me: 'You did well.' Not many people say that now that I'm a Cardinal! There's one other thing that's different about Gerard – he has Down's Syndrome.

If that abnormality were to be detected nowadays, his mother Joyce would be under intense pressure to have an abortion. Yet she'll tell you that Gerard has given so much more to their family than he's taken back. They can't imagine life without him.

Unfortunately today, most babies with the chromosome make-up of Gerard are killed in their mother's wombs.

I'm pro-life because of people like Brendan and Pauline Boland.

When they found they couldn't have children, they came to our adoption society to ask to be put on the list . . . and they waited, and waited and waited.

I would see them every year at the annual adoption Mass, but never with a baby.

Why? Because there were too few babies for too many couples.

Nowadays, abortion has replaced adoption as the logical conclusion of an unplanned pregnancy.

When I first became a bishop in 1971, our adoption society had 210 babies for placement annually. Last year they had four.

Brenda and Pauline's story does have a happy ending.

After five years, Anthony was placed with them and completed their lives. For many couples, though, the wait for a child will have no such happy ending.

I'm pro-life because of families like Eddie and Margaret McInnes. They came to me one night, five or six years ago, distraught because they had been told the baby they were expecting had a severe handicap and they had been advised to abort.

I offered to help in any way I could. I prayed and asked others to pray for them and I encouraged them to persevere.

You can imagine my joy and theirs when, a few months later, Alecia was born – healthy in every way.

It's because of people like these that I'm pro-life.

As a Church we don't only protest – in fact, I have no time for the violence employed by some so-called 'pro-lifers' in the United States. Instead, we prefer to help and counsel women in difficult circumstances who are pregnant.

In a quiet and discreet way we offer places for those who want to have their child away from their home area. We offer help to those who have had an abortion. We turn no one away.

Next month I'll be speaking to Shelter about the scandal of homelessness.

Most recently I've been looking at ways of opposing an apparent suggestion of an NHS agency that children should be handed out condoms at primary-school level.

Already they're handed over to young students at our universities. Surely, that can't be right.

I've campaigned for many years against the scandal of the arms race and I'll continue to campaign for people's rights to be respected as long as I'm able to do so.

But the most fundamental right of all is the right to life. Without it, no other right has any meaning.

That's why I'm pro-people. That's why I'm pro-life . . . in every way.

Nobel winner backs abortion 'for any reason'

By Steve Boggan, Glenda Cooper and Charles Arthur

The Nobel prize-winning scientist who unravelled the structure of DNA said yesterday that women should be able to abort foetuses at will if advances in genetics showed that they would be born gay, or dyslexic, or musically untalented or even too short to play basketball.

In an interview with *The Independent*, Dr James Watson said 'there could be 1,000 different reasons' why women might want to abort a child, 'many of them absurd', but society should do nothing to stop them.

Dr Watson was speaking from his home in New York following angry reaction to an article in the *Sunday Telegraph* published under the headline: 'Abort babies with gay genes, says Nobel winner.' He said last night that he intended to sue the newspaper for giving the impression that he advocated aborting babies if future advances in science led to testing for a gay gene, whereas he simply believes that mothers should have the right to abort foetuses for any reason.

His comments provoked outrage in the gay community and among pro-lifers.

However, his justification of them appeared to lead him into more extreme territory.

'During an interview, I was asked about homosexuality and I related a story about a woman who felt her life had been ruined because her son was a homosexual and she would never have grandchildren,' he said. 'I simply said that women in that situation should have a choice over whether or not to abort. I didn't say that foetuses found to have a gay gene should be aborted.' However, when asked where society should draw the abortion line, he replied: 'Society shouldn't . . . I don't see where you can draw the line. Some people might not want a child who is dyslexic. A woman could say that some day, if a gene were discovered for musical ability, and her child didn't have it, she might want to abort.

'Someone else might say, I do not want my child to be short because I love basketball and he'll be too short to play . . .' Gay rights groups and pro-lifers reacted angrily to Dr Watson's remarks.

Kathleen O'Hanlan, a leading gay researcher and activist at Stanford University in California said: 'Science doesn't designate homosexuality as a disease. Aborting a foetus for what is not a disease appears to be more like the practice of eugenics, more like the 1940s in Nazi Germany than the 1990s in the US or Britain. It will not be tolerated.' Professor Jack Scarisbrick, Director of the pro-life charity Life, said that the idea was a 'horrible suggestion. All abortion is an offence to the right to life of a child and a violation of a mother,' he said. 'To do this because an alleged gene is going to result in homosexuality is a terrible discrimination.'

Unwanted pregnancy and abortion

Some questions answered

Could I be pregnant?

If you have had sex without using a contraceptive or the contraceptive you use has failed, you could be pregnant.

'Morning-after' birth control can prevent an unwanted pregnancy if the woman is treated within 72 hours of unprotected sex. It is available from some doctors, Family Planning Clinics or Brook Advisory Centres. It is not an alternative to regular contraception but an emergency measure which can prevent an unwanted pregnancy.

What are the symptoms of pregnancy?

The most common sign of possible pregnancy is a missed period. Other signs are sickness, swollen breasts and passing urine more frequently.

What do I do if I miss my period?

If your period is a week overdue you should go for a pregnancy test. Your doctor should be able to do this. However, if you do not want to go to your doctor, go to your local Family Planning Clinic, Brook Advisory Centre, or buy a home-test kit from a chemist. It is important that you seek help as early as possible because if you decide you do not want to continue the pregnancy and you want to seek an abortion, the earlier it is done in the pregnancy the safer it is for you.

If your pregnancy test is negative but you miss another period you should have a repeat test.

If I am pregnant, what can I do?

There are three options open to you.

Firstly, even if the pregnancy is unplanned, you may decide to continue with it and have a child. If this is the case you should go to your doctor and arrange ante-natal care.

Secondly, you may decide to continue with the pregnancy and have the child adopted. Details of adoption agencies may be obtained from Citizens' Advice Bureaux, local social services, local churches, the Family Planning Association, etc.

Thirdly, you may decide to seek an abortion.

Who can I talk to?

Whatever your final decision you may want to discuss all the options with someone else. This could be your doctor or a counsellor at a Family Planning Clinic or Brook Advisory Centre. If you feel you can, you should discuss it with your parents, although you may be nervous of their reaction.

If you are under sixteen years of age and wish to seek an abortion your parents will normally need to be involved in the decision. If, however, you have strong reasons for not wanting them to know, the doctor is legally able to agree to the abortion without your parents' knowledge or consent so long as you show that you fully understand what it means to have an abortion.

What is an abortion?

An abortion is when a pregnancy is ended before a baby is capable of surviving on its own outside the mother's body. An abortion can either happen naturally, i.e. a miscarriage, or it can be induced, i.e. done deliberately. An induced abortion is only legal if it is carried out within the law and in the circumstances which the law permits.

Never attempt to induce an abortion yourself as this could cause you serious injury.

What does the law say about abortion?

Under the terms of the Abortion Act, a woman requires the agreement of two doctors before an abortion can be carried out. Doctors can agree to an abortion if they believe one or more of the following:

a) continuing with the pregnancy

would involve more risk to your physical or mental health than terminating it.

b) continuing with the pregnancy would involve greater risk to your life than terminating it.

c) any existing children of yours would be likely to suffer if the pregnancy continued.

d) there is a substantial risk that the child would be deformed or seriously handicapped.

A doctor can take into account your financial and social circumstances when considering your request for an abortion, if you are less than 24 weeks pregnant.

Where should I go if I decide to seek an abortion?

You should first go to your doctor. If the doctor agrees to your request you would normally be referred to a local NHS hospital and seen by another doctor who, if agreeable to the abortion, would make the arrangements for your admission to hospital.

In some cases (partly depending on where you live) NHS facilities may not be available for abortion and you may then be referred to either a non-profit-making clinic dealing with abortion or a private clinic. In these circumstances you may have to pay for the abortion.

What do I do if the doctor will not help me?

Some doctors do not agree with abortion, although they should refer you to another doctor. Other women for personal reasons may not wish to go to their doctor. In these circumstances you should go for help to one of the following: Family Planning Association, a Brook Advisory Centre, the British Pregnancy Advisory Service or a Citizens' Advice Bureau.

What does abortion involve?

If you are in the first twelve weeks of pregnancy the abortion will be a very simple operation performed under either local or general anaesthetic. If the abortion is carried out in a day care unit you could be out of hospital or clinic on the same day. In other places you may have to stay overnight. If you are later into the pregnancy, the simpler abortion techniques may not be possible and you will have to stay in hospital a little longer.

How can I reduce the risks of an unwanted pregnancy?

If you are having sex with a man and do not want a child, it is essential that you seek contraceptive advice and choose a method of contraception that suits you.

If you do not want to go to your own doctor, use your local Family Planning Clinic or Brook Advisory Centre. (Brook Advisory Centres give particular help to young people.)

Remember: If the contraceptive you use fails (i.e. a burst condom) or you forget to use your contraceptive, emergency contraception used within 72 hours of unprotected sex can prevent an unwanted pregnancy.

What is ALRA?

The Abortion Law Reform Association (ALRA)was formed in 1936 and was the major pressure group behind the Abortion Act.

ALRA supports a woman's right to choose whether or not to continue with a pregnancy and campaigns for further liberalisation of the law and for improved NHS facilities.

Public opinion

Public opinion towards abortion has become more liberal in recent years. In the British Social Attitudes Survey of 1983, 83% agreed that a woman should decide on her own that she does not wish to have the child, compared with 56% in 1990.[1]

In a 1995 MORI poll,[2] 66% of those questioned either strongly agreed or tended to agree with the principle of abortion on demand. This was backed up by a 1996 MORI poll[3] which showed that 58% of those questioned did not know that the law requires a women to secure the permission of two doctors before an abortion. When this was explained, 53% supported a change in the law to make abortion available on request in the first three months of pregnancy.

In the latest Northern Ireland survey,[4] 30% supported abortion at the request of the woman, 36% supported abortion in the case of extreme poverty, and 79% supported abortion if it was necessary to maintain the physical or mental health of the woman.

Doctor's attitudes

In a 1989[5] survey, 73% of consultant gynaecologists in Great Britain agreed that a woman should have the right to choose, in consultation with her doctor, whether to have an abortion. Fifteen per cent had a conscientious objection to abortion and this group were less likely to perform abortions over 12 weeks.

A similar survey[6] of gynaecologists in Northern Ireland showed that over two-thirds supported a change in the law which would leave the decision on whether to continue a pregnancy to the woman and her doctor. Half of the doctors surveyed said that they had a conscientious objection to abortion, although 95% would carry out an abortion in certain circumstances.

References

1 Jowell R et al eds. *British Social Attitudes: the 7th Report*. Gower, 1990.
2 MORI. *Public attitudes to abortion*. Birth Control Trust, 1995.
3 MORI. *Attitudes towards abortion*. Marie Stopes International and National Abortion Campaign, 1996.
4 Ulster Marketing Surveys Limited. *Birth control and abortion – a Northern Ireland opinion survey*, 1994.
5 Savage W and Francome C. 'Gynaecologists' attitudes to abortion'. *Lancet*, 2 December 1989, pp 1323-1324.
6 Francome C. 'Gynaecologists and abortion in Northern Ireland'. *Journal of Biosocial Science*, vol 26, 1994. pp 389-394.

• The above is an extract from Factsheet 13, *Abortion*, published by the Family Planning Association. See page 39 for address details.

A woman's right to choose?

Women and the problem pregnancy. We all know what abortion does to the unborn child. But there's one other very important person involved. The woman. What happens to her?

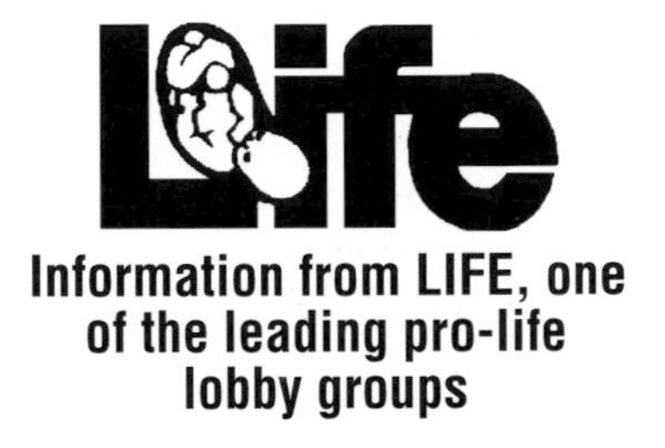

Information from LIFE, one of the leading pro-life lobby groups

What we are told

For over 25 years women in Britain were told that abortion was a safe little procedure, involving no big problems. Women needed abortion to have total control over their fertility and total freedom to choose what to do with their lives. Abortion would bring with it a new status for women. At last women would be equal with men because they would not have to bear unwanted children. So we were told.

Safe little procedure?

Abortion is invasive of women's bodies whatever method is used, whether surgical or chemical. Surgical methods can damage future fertility as well as cause immediate infection. Chemical abortion uses drugs that are immediately dangerous for some women, painful to use, and can have still-uncharted long-term effects on women's health.

After abortion women are more likely to miscarry or give birth prematurely.

No big problems?

Abortion causes more than physical damage to women. Abortion abuses women. It leaves many women filled with anger, guilt, regret, loss of self-esteem, and unable to trust others. Relationships often collapse after abortion, and many women are left with no man, no baby, and alienated parents. No one forgets an abortion.

For some women the strain of coping, often alone, with their feelings afterwards causes more problems than any posed by the unwanted pregnancy.

Total control over their fertility?

The number of unplanned pregnancies has risen steadily since abortion was legalised. This is despite free contraception for everyone, even under-age girls, since 1974. So what's happened to fertility control?

Readily available abortion means that, if conception occurs, the problem can be 'solved' at once. Inevitably there is more sexual activity at ever younger ages. No contraception, much of which is anyway abortifacient, is totally effective. So there are more and more unplanned pregnancies.

Freedom to choose?

When pregnancy is unwanted what real choice is there?

The choice is between abortion, with its physical and emotional after-effects, or continuing the pregnancy. Those people closely involved with the pregnant woman know that if pregnancy continues they will be expected to do something to help her and her baby. If she has an abortion they need do nothing. She has the abortion alone. She has to live with it afterwards – alone.

For selfish partners, parents, friends, the choice is simple. They do the choosing, not her. Sometimes the pressure is gentle. Often it isn't. There is little freedom of choice when those who should give love and support walk away leaving her to cope alone. Readily available abortion has made women more vulnerable.

Control over their lives?

Pregnancy changes a woman's life, whether or not it ends in abortion. It is possible to plan ahead when continuing pregnancy, and the problems and joys of motherhood can be foreseen. But abortion is a journey into the unknown. No one knows what she will feel like afterwards, either immediately or in the future. Many women are unprepared for the destructive effects of abortion on their lives.

Status of women

But, say the abortionists, it's necessary for the equal status of women that there is safe, legal abortion. Unless women can enjoy the same access to hassle-free sex that men, allegedly, have traditionally enjoyed for centuries, they will never be equal, never have the same chances as men.

Well, in Great Britain women have had 25 years of this chance of achieving equal status. What's happened?

A third of births are now to women who are not married. That may include women in a stable relationship who choose not to marry and have the full support of their partner in childrearing. But it undoubtedly includes many lone mothers who chose against abortion and find they have to cope alone.

Instead of the women enjoying the sexual freedom allegedly conferred by abortion it seems to be exactly what uncaring men like. If the man doesn't want to be involved he just says, 'It's your choice', and pushes off. Some women will then have an abortion but many won't because they know what abortion can do to them, and they appreciate the rights of the child.

A new underclass

These brave women often find that, apart from LIFE, not a lot of people are interested in helping them. The new poor in Britain include many lone mothers with young babies. Are they liberated? Is their status as mothers, as women, appreciated? No. Instead, they are criticised by Government and media pundits as a burden on society.

The enormous rise in divorce has damaged the status of many women. No one asks what the connection is between abortion and divorce. Why not? If most unmarried relationships break up after abortion, won't abortion also damage marriage? One-third of women having abortions are married. One-third of marriages end in divorce in Britain. Are the two facts connected?

New role-models

The status of women in their unique role as mothers and homemakers has never been so low. All the skills women were traditionally praised for and proud of – connected with family care and home-making – are officially rubbished by the abortion-driven propagandists. Female role-models we are invited to admire usually include women who support abortion, reject children or cannot sustain a relationship.

And where is the enhanced status of women in the visual arts, media, literature? There has never been more violence and pornography directed at and involving women – as well as children. What is the connection between abortion and the way in which women are routinely portrayed even on prime-time television – the rapes, the beatings, the foul language, the sheer vulgarity?

Violence

Abortion itself violates women. And the message that violence is acceptable to women has bred dangerously.

Easy abortion makes women's bodies finally available for sex, with (apparently) no fear of the consequences, and the approval of the chattering classes. So what's wrong in taking the violence and disposability ever further?

The truly pro-woman way

LIFE has for over 20 years counselled and helped hundreds of thousands of women and their families with the problems caused by unwanted pregnancy or abortion. Most members of LIFE are women, with extensive experience of the fears, wishes, hopes of women. LIFE knows that abortion 'solves' nothing, usually leaves women in the same difficult situation as before, and often does such damage to the health of women that they are worse off than ever.

LIFE's free, confidential care for women provides a better way forward in even the most difficult situation: even where pregnancy results from rape, incest or abuse, or the unborn child has been diagnosed as disabled.

LIFE gives help that accepts and respects women and their babies.

LIFE's is the truly pro-woman way.

Hard questions answered

Information from LIFE

. . . backstreet abortions?

This term is usually used for illegal abortions which are not performed in hospitals or clinics.

Even before the Abortion Act, the number of women in danger after backstreet abortions was getting fewer. It is, of course, impossible to produce accurate figures for such illegal activities, but the numbers of women admitted to hospital after botched abortions was on the way down years before 1967.

Backstreet abortions were almost always performed early in pregnancy. The development of the child makes later abortions impossible to perform without medical facilities.

Those who think abortion is wrong reject backstreet abortions along with all other abortions. It is not where, or how badly, they are performed that makes the difference. Wherever or however they are performed, at least one life is ended, sometimes two. And to argue that we must legalise abortion because there will always otherwise be an illegal backstreet trade is like saying that we must legalise bad driving because there will always be bad drivers. If people are being beaten up in the backstreets should we establish clinics where they can be attacked in hygienic conditions? Of course not.

. . . when the child is disabled?

Tests are now available to detect disability in the womb from about 10 weeks into pregnancy. The principal tests are:

Chorionic villus sampling (CVS) – not widely available, this tests a tiny part of the placenta very early in pregnancy.

Alpha-feto protein test (AFP) – widely used, this involves testing a blood sample from the mother at about 16 weeks.

Amniocentesis test – generally available, this involves removing some of the amniotic fluid from around the child by syringe from about 18 weeks.

Ultrasound scanning – quite generally available, as well as a useful tool in dating the pregnancy, ultrasound can reveal the development of the child by 'bouncing' soundwaves off the baby to produce a moving picture on the screen of a monitor.

However and whenever disability is detected, the child needs help with the difficulties and the family needs support. Abortion does not prevent or help disability. It kills the disabled. Acceptance of abortion on these grounds has led to the killing of newborn disabled children who are unwanted or rejected. To kill a child because he or she is disabled strikes many people as particularly cruel and unfair.

Moreover, prenatal screening is not wholly reliable. It is reckoned that 10% of diagnoses by ultrasound machines are wrong. Other tests may reveal spina bifida, for instance, but cannot predict the degree of disability in the born child. As well as resulting in healthy children being put to death, amniocentesis (like CVS) can seriously damage children in the womb and has a 1% chance of causing miscarriage.

Disabled children are still human beings. Should we discriminate against them? We are all disabled to some extent!

. . . abortion after rape?

Conception can result from rape, but this is rare. There are surveys covering thousands of cases of rape which report no pregnancy. But it does sometimes happen.

Whether or not pregnancy has resulted, the raped woman needs a lot of help to recover from the terrible experience.

In deciding whether abortion can be part of this help, we must remember that abortion is itself a violation of a woman, and that many women are damaged by it. Some women suffer terribly from post-abortion syndrome which means that an abortion following rape may add to the woman's problems rather than help her recover from them.

While some might think that continuing the pregnancy will remind the woman of the rape, experience often tells a different story. Some women in this situation accept the child as something good coming out of something awful, and want to keep the child and not, for example, give it away for adoption.

The child, of course, is innocent of any guilt and is just like any other child. It seems unfair to punish the child, condemning him/her to death, because of his/her father's crime. The violence of abortion is no solution to the violence of rape.

. . . abortion to save the life of the mother

In years gone by, we are told, the choice between saving the mother or the child was not uncommon. Medical knowledge and science have advanced in recent years to such an extent that this need not be the case in our own days.

There are nowadays a few occasions when the life of the mother is threatened by the pregnancy. This is normally late in pregnancy and, of course, the pregnancy must be ended, otherwise both mother and child will die. But there is no reason to perform an abortion and thereby kill the child. The child can be delivered (by surgery) and given a chance to survive. Children delivered a little over half-way through pregnancy now have a much better chance of survival because of the skill of doctors and the facilities available in Special Care Baby Units.

In this rare situation good medicine can save both mother and baby, and there is no need to kill one or the other.

Key facts

The following information came from *Key Facts About Legalised Abortion In Britain*, published by the Society for the Protection of Unborn Children (SPUC)

- **Since the Abortion Act came into force in April 1968, more than four and a half million unborn children have been killed in Britain under the Abortion Act.**

In 1995, 163,621 abortions – 448 a day – were done in England and Wales[1], and 11,316 – 30 a day – in Scotland.[2]

- **Over 90% of abortions are done for 'social' reasons.**

The most frequently cited ground for abortion refers to 'risk of injury to the physical or mental health of the pregnant woman,' of which the Royal College of Obstetricians and Gynaecologists has said: 'there is no such danger of injury in the majority of these cases as the 'indication' is purely a social one.'[3]

In 1990, pro-abortion MP Emma Nicholson referred to 'the fiction that the 1967 Act does not provide abortions on request – of course it does . . . General practitioners in my constituency and elsewhere tell me that it is virtually impossible for a doctor to refuse an abortion under the workings of the 1967 Act.'[4]

Only a tiny fraction of one per cent of abortions have been performed in emergency for the stated reasons of saving the mother's life or preventing grave permanent injury to her health. In 1995, only one such abortion was preformed in Scotland, and none in England and Wales.

- **Abortion is now legal up to birth on grounds of handicap.**

Abortion is also legal on grounds which permit some 'social' abortions. In 1995, 'substantial risk of the child being born seriously handicapped' was a ground cited in 1,868 abortions in England and Wales; 130 in Scotland. In England and Wales, a total of 73 abortions were performed at 25 weeks gestation and over; more than three times the annual number of post-24 week abortions before abortion up to birth came into force in 1991. There were 5 post 24-week abortions in Scotland.

References: 1 Abortions statistics for England and Wales are taken from the publications of the Office for National Statistics. Figured for 1995 are taken from the monitor AB 96/5. 2 Abortions statistics for Scotland are published by the Information and Statistics Division of the Scottish Health Service. At the time of writing, figures for 1995 are provisional and were reported verbally to the SPUC Scottish Office on request. 3 Royal College of Obstetricians and Gynaecologists, first report on *Unplanned Pregnancy*, 1972. 4 Hansard 24 April 1990, cols 249/250.

Abortion

A position statement from the Family Planning Association (FPA)

Background

The founding principle of the Family Planning Association was, and remains, 'every child a wanted child' – access to contraception has freed millions of women from the misery of being unable to determine whether and when to bear children, and from consequent poverty and ill-health. Research shows that most heterosexually active women and men use contraception most of the time; research also shows that over 30%, and perhaps as many as 50%, of pregnancies in Britain are unintentional.

To be effective in preventing pregnancy, contraceptives must be easily accessible and acceptable to users. Many contraceptives currently available are highly effective; none is 100% effective, even when used with care and consistency. Contraceptive methods themselves do fail, while emergency (post-coital) contraception is neither widely advertised nor readily accessible. There are also a multitude of psychological, social and economic factors which contribute to the incidence of unplanned or unwanted pregnancy.

There are also many factors which influence a woman's perception of her pregnancy and of her ability to care for a child. For many women an unplanned pregnancy becomes wanted, resulting in a wanted child; some women choose to continue the pregnancy and place the child for adoption. Others choose to end the pregnancy – surveys currently show that one in five of all pregnancies in Britain is ended by abortion.

The 1967 Abortion Act made abortion legal under defined circumstances in Britain; this Act of Parliament does not extend to Northern Ireland where abortion is still not legal under most circumstances. The current provision of abortion services within the National Health Service in Britain is best described as inconsistent, varying in quality, availability and accessibility. For some women, obtaining a Health Service abortion is extremely difficult, no matter how early their pregnancy is detected, how quickly they seek help and regardless of their legal entitlement. Many women must choose between trying to gain access to Health Service facilities or paying for abortion.

The FPA's primary aim is to educate for sexual well-being, reproductive health and planned parenthood; the Association also recognises that access to abortion remains a healthcare priority. The FPA maintains that high-quality abortion services are a necessary and integral part of family planning provision within the Health Service, notwithstanding the availability and accessibility of contraceptive methods. The FPA supports the work of other pro-choice organisations in improving the accessibility and quality of abortion services in Britain, and supports the right of women to choose abortion.

FPA statement

1. The FPA supports the right of women to choose abortion, and to have access to services which offer early, safe and effective treatment, with sympathetic care throughout.
2. The FPA believes that the 1967 Abortion (Amended) Act should be extended to Northern Ireland.
3. Every woman with an unintended pregnancy has the right to be offered complete, accurate and impartial information, and to be treated non-judgementally and with respect. The woman's care, counselling and access to services should not be prejudiced by her social circumstances, the religious beliefs of others, financial considerations, cultural background, disability, sexuality, previous

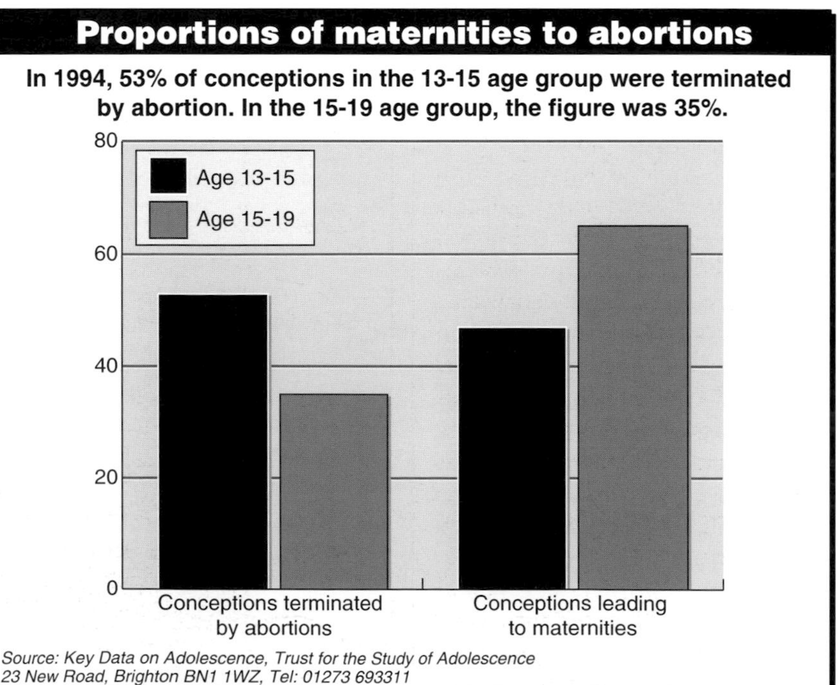

Source: Key Data on Adolescence, Trust for the Study of Adolescence 23 New Road, Brighton BN1 1WZ, Tel: 01273 693311

gynaecological history or health status of the woman or foetus.

4 Free pregnancy diagnosis should be readily available within primary healthcare facilities, supported by counselling services for woman and men who require them, and efficient systems for onward referral where necessary.

5 The preparedness of GPs to refer adult and adolescent women for abortion must be made clear in their practice leaflet. GPs who are unwilling to refer for abortion must advise women of their right to go to another GP without re-registration. Direct referral for abortion should also be available from Family Planning Clinics, particularly for women who use those clinics for contraceptive services.

6 Inaccessible services, poor communication and administrative delays result in termination being performed later than necessary, or being refused, despite prompt and responsible action by the woman. Pregnancy diagnosis, referral systems and clinical practice should facilitate the ideal of abortion on request in the first trimester of pregnancy, and the option of self-referral to abortion services.

7 Whilst supporting initiatives intended to ensure that abortion is most often carried out within the first trimester of pregnancy, the FPA will not support any proposals for lowering the legal time limit for abortion.

8 No individual, organisation or agency has the right to veto a woman's choice of legal abortion, to coercively persuade against a woman's right to choose abortion or to obstruct access to services to which she is legally entitled.

9 The FPA believes that abortion services are best provided by individuals and organisations who regard the sympathetic provision of abortion services as a positive contribution to health and well-being. District Health Authorities who are unable to offer an appropriate level of service should enter into contracts with specialist agencies providing abortion care in order to maintain service provision and accessibility within that District. Health professionals should continue to have the right to refuse directly to take part in abortion services, provided that their refusal does not put at risk the physical or mental well-being of women who choose abortion.

10 The FPA supports the continued development and evaluation of medical methods of abortion, such as anti-progestins with prostaglandin procedures. Medical abortion offers the possibility of community-based family planning provision which includes abortion services; the FPA would support such provision if safety, efficacy and acceptability studies show this to be appropriate.

11 It must not be assumed that a woman who undergoes pregnancy screening, or diagnostic testing, will agree to abortion regardless of the result of the test. Under no circumstances should access to such services be conditional on agreement to abortion, regardless of the woman's reasons for requesting/agreeing to antenatal testing.

12 In the event of foetal disability the woman and her partner, where appropriate, should be offered full and impartial information about the nature of the disability, its likely prognosis and implications, and any care and assistance services available. Information-giving and non-directive coun-selling must be differentiated, and offered by appropriately trained and experienced personnel.

13 Women and men who wish to explore options other than abortion should be offered counselling and support, including information about adoption, foster-care, and relevant statutory, non-statutory and self-help services and organisations for parents and children.

14 Counselling by appropriately qualified personnel must be available and accessible to all women who request or who have experienced abortion, and to their partners. Such services must be sensitive and supportive, with regard to the implications of abortion for, and the needs of, both women and men.

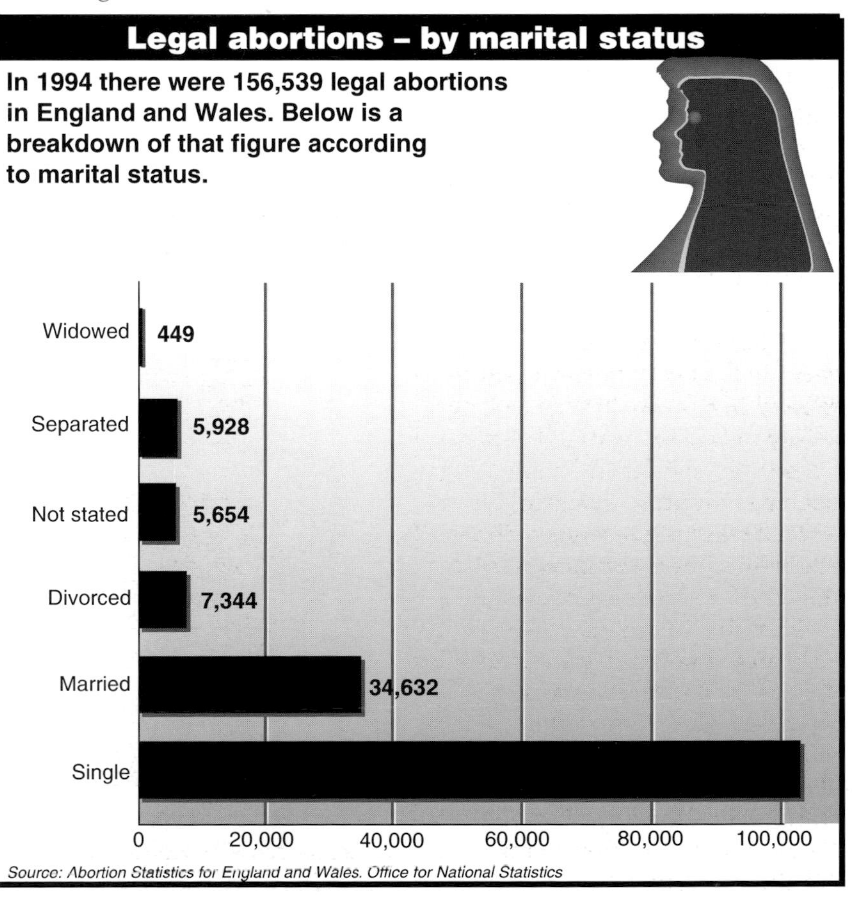

Crying shame of the past

Camilla Roskelly warns the pro-life lobby to think again before calling for laws that could kill desperate women

As a young woman of about 20, I had a backstreet abortion. I was boarding school (mainly convent) educated; my father had been away during the Second World War and my mother working. On father's return, my parents found they'd grown apart, and after a while, to my relief, they separated.

I eloped with a man 15 years my senior. My parents tried to stop me – but hell, their marriage had broken up, what did they know? As it happened, my mate was soon revealed to be a violent, alcoholic gambler. One night, he came home after several days' absence, blacked my eyes (again) and vomited over my sleeping first-born son. I realised that love could not conquer quite all and left him.

But in custody proceedings, he gained access to my son, and on a visit to see him, my husband raped me. It was not done out of love or even lust, but as women are raped in war, as an expression of domination and hatred. I became pregnant with the fruit of his hatred and my humiliation.

After agonising for some time, I decided to seek an abortion. Abortions were illegal. I don't think I had actually realised that such a procedure existed before I found myself in desperate need of it.

My father had taken me in when I fled the 'matrimonial home'. I did not perceive it as my right to sully his doorstep any more than I already had done, nor did I perceive it as my right to make him in any way complicit with an illegal act. Telling him, consulting with him beforehand, would in my mind have tainted him with such complicity.

So I did not discuss my pregnancy with him, nor what had led up to it, nor even what I intended to do about it. I loved, and love, both my parents.

I raised the money, and found out where to go for the abortion. It was a small house, in a backstreet terrace. I slunk there, ashamed, convinced that everyone was watching me, that everyone knew, that the police would come and drag me off to prison for my wickedness.

So would you put young women like me back on that grubby kitchen table?

A woman wearing a pinafore opened the door and showed me into her kitchen. I remember the brown linoleum and the grubby, wooden kitchen table on which I lay. I remember the white enamel bowl, blue-rimmed, from which a douche of soap and water was squirted into my cervix and I felt a pain such as I had never before experienced, even in childbirth.

'Don't talk about it,' said the woman. 'It's illegal. Don't go to hospital. They'll find out, and we'll both be in trouble. It's murder, you know. When it starts to happen, you must put up with it. It'll come away eventually.'

But I had to return and have the whole grisly act performed again, because it didn't 'come away' first time.

When at last it did happen, it happened with a vengeance. I had such a haemorrhage that I could no longer crawl from my bedroom to the lavatory, and lay bleeding in the corridor. I still did not tell my father, who found me and took me to hospital just in time to save my life; I did not want to involve him in illegality. And I still have not told him about it. He might have guessed, but the subject remains undiscussed.

Today, prominent and well-meaning people, moral people, are telling us not to vote for a candidate who is not anti-abortion. But I believe that to treat a desperate affair like abortion as a simplistic election issue is to devalue a decision which, for anyone who has had to make it, is too personal, too intimate, too enduringly hurtful to be used as a peg for dogma.

I also deeply believe the sexual act should be an expression of mutual love, responsibility, passion and fun. It should consolidate a relationship and if a loved and wanted child is the result, well and good. But not all relationships are like that.

Of course, no one wants to kill or harm babies; that is the reason for contraception. But the logical consequence of following electoral advice from the cardinals and others would be to make abortion once more illegal.

So would you put young women like me back on that grubby kitchen table?

So would you put young women like me back on that grubby kitchen table?

A campaign to abort

In Britain, tighter laws are not the best way to limit the use of abortion

Doctrinaire 'pro-lifers' will not agree, but Britain's Abortion Act, 30 years old in 1997, has served the country well. Formally, it allows abortion where two doctors certify that a continued pregnancy would risk the health of mother or child. Informally, it is interpreted liberally so that most pregnant women who are adamant that they do not want a child can get safe legal terminations. Abortion is thus primarily a matter for the individual conscience, within a flexible framework of law determined by a free, rather than partisan, vote of the House of Commons.

True, the British solution involves an element of fudge. It has therefore never satisfied those who endorse a woman's unfettered right to choose, nor those who oppose all abortion on principle. In the run-up to the 1997 general election, the latter 'pro-lifers' have suddenly become unusually active, threatening to run candidates against 'pro-choice' MPs. Big guns among Britain's Catholic hierarchy have lent support to their objectives.

This is not a happy development. In countries where abortion has become a conventional political battleground, the fighting has invariably been nasty.

America is divided over abortion, with pro-lifers harassing and even attacking nurses and doctors as well as unsympathetic politicians. Abortion has unsettled usually-harmonious Germany, where the west has traditionally been restrictive, the east liberal. From Poland to South Africa, fierce arguments rage between uncompromising opponents.

The campaign is also probably pointless-although it is making pro-choice MPs with small majorities nervous. Parliament did vote overwhelmingly in 1990 to cut the time limit for legal abortions from 28 weeks to 24 weeks to reflect the earlier viability of the foetus under modern medicine. But today, British opinion polls show clear majority support for the legal status quo. Even among Catholics a majority opposes change. Most MPs are therefore minded to leave well alone.

In the Netherlands, which is liberal on abortion and active in sex education, the abortion rate is lower than in almost all other western countries

An anti-abortion strategy

It is not as if the abortion rate in Britain is particularly high. For 15 years it has been stable at around 170,000-190,000 a year. This compares favourably with rates in many other western countries, and particularly with America. Given the modern pressures – for example, on women who wish to make their careers before they start their families – some upward movement in numbers might be expected. It is good news that little such movement has taken place.

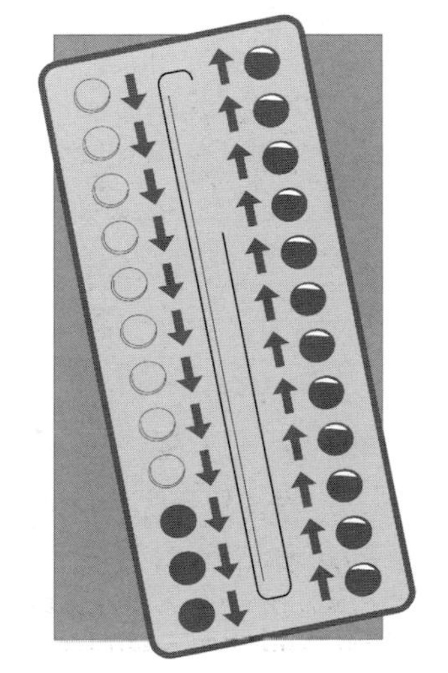

If abortions could be reduced further without limiting individual choice, so much the better. There is little mystery as to how this might be achieved: by better sex education combined with ready availability of contraception.

In schools in America where this has been provided, teenagers become sexually active at a later age. One study, carried out in Baltimore by Laurie Zabin, a public health researcher, found that teenage pregnancies fell by 30%. In the Netherlands, which is liberal on abortion and active in sex education, the abortion rate is lower than in almost all other western countries. The ready availability of contraception also helps to avoid an outcome that both sides should consider undesirable: the use of abortion as a conventional sort of family planning. Unfortunately, the Catholic Church (if not most of its British flock) opposes contraception as well as abortion. And many pro-lifers are squeamish about sex education, too.

This is a pity. Pro-lifers are wasting their efforts in trying to get Britain's abortion laws changed in ways that most of the population do not support. Yet there is an alternative: to work with the grain of public opinion, accept that abortion will remain legal and campaign instead for more sensible sex education and better contraception. In this they would be enthusiastically supported by pro-choicers: an unlikely alliance, but one that really could secure the reduction in abortions they claim to want.

The abortion debate

This law is about need, not demand, says a doctor. Despite medical arguments, most people agree money worries play a part. Celia Hall reports

Every year in England and Wales there are nearly 160,000 abortions. Latest figures show that numbers rose by 14.5 per cent in the spring and summer of last year following doubts about the safety of the Pill.

Thousands of women stopped taking the Pill after a warning in October 1995 by the Department of Health that seven brands of commonly-used contraceptives had a slightly higher risk of causing thrombosis.

Nearly half of the women who had abortions have no other children; more than 100,000 of them were single; 35,000 were married and the rest were divorced or separated or their status was unknown.

Nearly 110,000 were between 20 and 34 in 1995, according to the most recent available breakdown of the data. More than 90 per cent of these abortions are allowed under the 1967 Abortion Act, when two doctors sign a statement saying that the pregnancy risks the 'mental or physical' health of the woman.

There is not much argument today that abortion up to the 24th week of the pregnancy is easily available for women who do not want to have the baby.

Despite the fraught debate that surrounds abortion there is one area where there is little argument.

There is agreement that panic about money and how to support the baby is almost always uppermost in the mind of the woman faced with the confirmation of an unplanned pregnancy.

Many doctors have become uneasy about the wide availability of abortion although there is little appetite within the medical profession to take on the debate.

Dr Sandy Macara, chairman of the British Medical Association, is

prepared to voice this apprehension.

'The Act was never intended to provide abortion on demand,' he said yesterday.

'What does worry a lot of us is the polarisation, being forced into positions which are pro-life or pro-choice.

'That is a shocking situation when what we should be considering in every individual case are the best interests of every mother and every baby. There is no doubt in my mind that lack of money plays a big part.

'We have all seen desperate women, pregnant again, who hear the cries of their hungry children with not enough food in their stomachs.

'What we should be able to do is to balance all the considerations to see how we can best help women – to get women the help they really need.

'The Abortion Act was about need and not about demand,' he said.

Some practical help does exist for women who specifically decide to go ahead with their pregnancies.

The charity Life runs 44 houses for women without support who want to have their babies.

Many doctors have become uneasy about the wide availability of abortion although there is little appetite within the medical profession to take on the debate

Local authorities pay the women's housing benefit directly to Life and the organisation helps the women to claim their personal state benefits.

At any time the charity is housing about 200 women who stay for nine months to a year, before and after their babies are born.

It is also planning to run a small number of 'next stage' flats for women with toddlers.

In addition it has its 'Gemma Fund' based on an Italian programme, which can provide immediate financial help in a crisis.

Last week it sent £150 to a pregnant woman whose boyfriend was out of work.

'The bills were piling up and they were short of food. This was a king's ransom to this family,' said Prof Jack Scarisbrick, the chairman of Life.

'We gave another woman who was expecting triplets £75 to buy a buggy.' Prof Scarisbrick said, however, that the charity would not be blackmailed.

It does not help women who say they will abort their baby unless Life gives them money.

'There is no doubt in my mind that economic pressure – even if it is imagined rather than real – is part of the panic that a woman experiences, and abortion thrives on fear,' he said.

'She thinks she won't be able to cope. Her mother says, "You won't be able to cope, dear".

'A little money at the right time as well as other support just gives a woman time – helps her to cool down a bit and not rush into a decision,' he said.

Life receives 90,000 calls a year on its counselling and advice line: 01926 311511.

The abortion lifeline

Call us for cash help, Catholics tell women in birth 'bribe' row

By Tom Fullerton and Jason Burt

The Roman Catholic Church is to set up a telephone hotline for women responding to an offer of financial help in return for cancelling an abortion.

Cardinal Thomas Winning's promise of assistance has prompted cash pledges of more than £50,000 from supporters keen to back his pro-life drive.

The leader of Scotland's Catholics issued an 'open invitation to any woman, any family, any couple', regardless of religion or background, to contact his archdiocese for help in a speech yesterday to a Glasgow conference of the Society for the Protection of Unborn Children.

His spokesman said that a £50,000 cash offer had been made by one man, with a woman also promising a share of the proceeds from the sale of her house.

'We have not made an appeal, but we expect many more people to come forward and respond in a similar manner,' he said.

The offer won immediate support from Cardinal Basil Hume, Archbishop of Westminster and leader of Catholics in England and Wales, who said that abortion was 'one of the greatest scandals of our time'.

It drew an angry rebuke, however, from pro-choice groups, who dismissed it as a 'cheap stunt' which was highly irresponsible.

The Birth Control Trust said it was appalled by Cardinal Winning's attempt to 'bribe' women.

Spokesman David Nolan said: 'These bribes are an empty gesture which ignore the reality of why women need access to abortion services and why women have abortions.' Cardinal Winning said that the resources of the Archdiocese of Glasgow – including financial help – would be opened up to any caller from today.

'Whatever worries or cares you may have, we will help you,' he said.

'If you need financial assistance, or help with equipment for your baby and feel financial pressures will force you to have an abortion, we will help you.' He refused to be drawn on exactly how his initiative would work or how much money was being made available to discourage women from 'making one of the biggest mistakes in your life'.

A flood of approaches would undoubtedly put a great strain on the cash-starved archdiocese.

But officials pointed to the flood of cash offers that flowed in last year following reports that a woman expecting twins insisted that she could not cope with two more babies and planned to abort one.

The anti-abortion group Life said it had been promised £10,000 in donations for a fund to help persuade women not to go ahead with abortions.

The Abortion Law Reform Association, which campaigns for women to have terminations on demand during the first three months of pregnancy, claimed the Cardinal was putting 'unfair pressure on women'.

The Church will welcome the publicity surrounding the offer as a way of once again putting moral issues high on the political agenda.

Cardinal Winning has already accused Labour leader Tony Blair of washing his hands of the issue by leaving the matter to the consciences of individual MPs.

The Labour Party last night refused to be drawn on the debate. A spokesman said Mr Blair considered it was a matter for the Church.

About 160,000 abortions were carried out in England and Wales last year.

More than half the babies born ten years from now could be delivered by caesarean section – at huge cost to the NHS, a leading obstetrician is warning.

Currently about 16 per cent of babies are delivered by caesarean but Professor Nicholas Fisk said he believed more and more women would opt for the 'safe' operation.

An Audit Commission report to be published next week will show it costs about £360 for a natural birth, while a caesarean can cost up to £1,100, according to BBC 1's *Here and Now* programme.

Professor Fisk, of Queen Charlotte's and Chelsea Hospital in London, tells the programme: 'I feel the trend will go up rather than down because of the patient choice issue and the prevention of damage to the baby and to the mother's pelvis, and because it is such a safe thing to do.'

A little money won't change their minds!

Julia Clarke asks whether the cash-for-kids offer can really work

Cardinal Thomas Winning has thrown the cat among the pigeons again with his latest bid to alter the abortion agenda.

But the big question behind his offer of cash to stop girls from aborting their babies is who will really pick up the tab? For, despite offers of short-term help from the Cardinal, the reality is the cost of more single mums would have to be met by the state.

Expense is certainly a factor which encourages some desperate young girls to decide to get rid of their babies.

The average family spends £90,000 raising their children. Families with one child spend an average of £64 a week, those with two spend £109 and those with three spend £130.

A study into teenage pregnancy in Tayside in 1993 shows conception is higher in the most deprived areas and the abortion rate much lower.

It is not the best-educated girls from advantaged families who fall pregnant young. If they do, they are more likely to choose abortion.

Young girls who decide to keep their babies are more likely to be disadvantaged to start with, with few job prospects and qualifications.

There is evidence some girls are choosing single motherhood as a 'career' – not just as a ticket to a house and benefits but because it's the one thing no one can take away from them.

This is particularly the case since there is now little stigma attached to motherhood outside marriage.

The girls whose minds Cardinal Winning is trying to change belong to a more privileged group, with more to lose if caught in the 'benefit trap' of single motherhood.

And it will take a lot more than some temporary support and a second-hand pram to change their minds. Though the Catholic Church disputes it, their flock appears less anti-abortion than ever before.

A poll last month found 50 per cent of Catholics support the right for some abortion.

There were 11,500 abortions in Scotland in 1995, with professional women in their early twenties the most likely to terminate pregnancies.

Most are performed on the NHS, with Tayside having the highest abortion rate. Will a handout from the Church really change that? Father Noel Barry, the Cardinal's press secretary, echoed Cardinal Winning's statement when he said: 'If you need financial assistance or help with equipment for your baby, and feel financial pressure will force you to have an abortion, we will help you.' But he warned: 'It doesn't mean we are talking about blank cheques or handing out bunches of fivers.

'We have moved from abortion on demand to abortion on offer.

'There is pressure on women to choose abortion and we say there is a need for practical alternatives, which of course do cost money.' Father Barry confirmed there would be no new fund set up by the church to finance pregnant women, though he would not rule out setting one up if the demand were there.

He said: 'Already we have received the offer of £50,000 and an offer from someone selling their house who has promised us some of the proceeds.

'If we need it, the money will be found.' On the charge that the church were 'pulling a cheap stunt', Father Barry said the only intention was to focus attention on a silent scandal.

He said: 'We want politicians to provide more resources to encourage women to keep their babies.

'We are not trying to make women feel guilty. But I would rather be accused of political manoeuvring than indifference.'

Catholics back pro-choice abortion stance

By Paul Riddell

More than two-thirds of Scottish Catholics believe women should have the right to choose abortion, according to new research out today.

And despite the fact that the Catholic Church outlaws abortion, a mere 22% take a pro-life stance.

In a System Three poll conducted for the BBC's *Frontline Scotland* programme, 68% of Catholics say they are pro-choice.

A mere 20% of those interviewed say they would vote for a candidate who opposed the right of a woman to choose whether to continue her pregnancy.

And almost twice as many say they would be less likely to vote for such a candidate.

But significantly, a third of Catholics say it would make no difference to their vote.

And in an apparent rebuke to Cardinal Thomas Winning, who last year provoked an 'unholy row' by criticising Labour's attitude towards abortion, the poll also found 51% of Catholics believe the Church should not comment on political issues.

The issue – on which Pope John Paul II has adopted a hardline stance – looks set to feature in the General Election as the anti-abortion Pro Life Alliance is to field 10 candidates in Scotland, particularly in Labour-held seats.

The single-issue group is targeting seats of those MPs who it believes have a bad record on abortion.

According to the programme, 'Faith, Votes and Sanctity', 25 years ago eight out of 10 Catholics in Scotland supported Labour – a figure which had fallen to five out of 10 at the last election.

Cardinal Winning accused Labour of 'inconsistency' and added: 'New Labour does have a number of Christian politicians and yet it has consistently avoided condemning abortion . . . and I don't believe that you can just brush aside the absolute right to life and be prepared to stand up for other rights that are less important than that.' And Catholic spokesman Father Noel Barry defended the Cardinal's stance, which drew fire from Labour ranks. And he denied that the Church is in the business of telling people how to vote.

John Maxton, Labour MP for Glasgow Cathcart, one of the seats targeted by the Alliance, said abortion ought to be a matter of individual conscience.

'What we want is to give people a choice of having an abortion and [in] having an abortion ensure that they have it safely,' he said.

And he claimed Catholics listen to Cardinal Winning when he talks about the Church but not when he addresses social issues.

Dr David McCrone, of Edinburgh University, claimed that the Church no longer carries the political influence it may once have had.

'If there was a point at which priests or ministers or religious figures did have much greater authority to speak from the pulpit and to convince the faithful that they should do something then those days are long gone,' he said.

'People are now much more proactive, much more sceptical, much more willing to think things out for themselves, and there is a lot of evidence that in this respect the Catholic population is no different from the rest of the population of Scotland.' But Bruno Quintavalle, of the Pro Life Alliance, said: 'I think that abortionism and a whole disrespect for life is having an evil influence on this country.

'Slowly it is corroding our basic values, turning our society into something which it really shouldn't be.' And he said the System Three poll illustrates the urgency of the task faced by his party.

'I think one has to be very clear about this, that anyone who truly is a Catholic will make abortion the priority issue in this election.' However, Liz Armstrong, of the Scottish Abortion Campaign, warned against making abortion a 'political football'.

'I think the issue of abortion, the choice that a woman has to make on her own, with her partner, with her family, is a very personal choice, and she must exercise her choice in the best way she can,' she said.

February, 1997

Abortion

As the shouting grows louder, is anyone listening to pregnant women? Ros Wynne-Jones investigates the 'counselling' offered at clinics by pros and antis and finds both sides wanting

A young mother is struggling with pushchair, shopping and wriggling infant on a London Underground escalator. Behind her are a series of posters advertising free pregnancy tests and advice at a drop-in centre close by.

Scrawled on one in lipstick are the words: 'BIASED, Don't Go.' The posters belong to Life, the anti-abortion charity.

As the spin doctors grapple for votes in the last weeks before the general election, another, more bloody, propaganda war is being waged over the familiar territory of the womb. Last night the newly-formed Pro Life Alliance party accused the National Abortion Campaign of a 'dirty-tricks initiative' aimed at discrediting both the Alliance and Life, the anti-abortion charity, by alleging that the two have links that violate Life's charitable status.

In the past week, with the pledge of Cardinal Thomas Winning, head of the Roman Catholic Church in Scotland, to halt the 'slaughter of the innocents' still ringing in their ears, the pro-choice and anti-abortion lobbies have both launched new offensives aimed at capturing the moral and political high ground.

The Pro Life Alliance has unveiled its manifesto for the election and will announce its first 50 candidates on Wednesday. In a counter-offensive, the National Abortion Campaign has begun a two-pronged attack on the anti-abortionists, organising a 'Speak Out' on 12 April to show how 'women have been empowered by taking control of their reproductive lives', and the campaign aimed at losing Life its charitable status.

The Alliance calls the NAC despicable; the NAC say the Catholic Church is attempting to bribe women not to have abortions; the Catholic Church talks of slaughter and genocide and the murder of unborn infants; abortion clinics talk of women's rights over their own bodies.

The propaganda battle is being fought in earnest over the airwaves, on poster hoardings and on the Internet. But, as in any conflict, there are inevitable casualties. In this one they are the women whom the pro-choice and anti-abortion lobbies are trying to save from each other, the pregnant women who for whatever reason are unsure about whether they want to be mothers.

Nowhere is the propaganda itself more chillingly blatant than on the frontline, in the advice centres where vulnerable women go for counselling.

Last week I followed the directions on one of the Underground posters offering free pregnancy tests and advice to a central London backstreet. The heavy door to Life is protected by a wire grille, grim testimony to the potential violence of the abortion war. Inside there are no hints that you have walked into a charity which is fundamentally opposed to abortion, just as there is none on the poster.

I decline a free pregnancy test, saying I've already had one and I just want to talk. I say my name's Jo, I'm 20 years old and eight weeks pregnant. I'm a student at a nearby university living on £2,000 a year, the baby is the product of a one-night stand, I don't want to tell the father and I can't tell my parents. Despite its anti-abortion agenda, Life is bound by law to give me non-directional counselling.

My counsellor is an anxious, earnest woman who unlocks another door to a standard-issue counselling room with comfy chairs, nondescript prints on the walls and a strategic box of tissues next to the seat I'm ushered into.

She starts off in a non-direction: 'It really depends how you feel about abortion . . .' but the end of her first sentence gives the lie to its beginning. Within five minutes I'm told that at eight weeks my baby's got eyes, its heart has started to beat and it's about the size of the palm of the counsellor's hand. I remember from biology lessons at school that the latter simply isn't true.

I hear about the guilt of 'post-abortion syndrome', the scarring that 'many women' suffer, leaving them unable to conceive again, how I will have to bear the secret of my abortion alone for the rest of my life. She looks pained as she tells me how they don't always get all the foetus out and sometimes leave a little hand behind and that can lead to trouble in later life.

Life can't give me any money 'because we rely on jumble sales and we don't have much', but they may be able to offer a second-hand pram, some baby clothes and a 'Moses basket'. They may even have room in one of their safe houses where I could stay until at least a year after the little one is born.

I'm handed a bunch of leaflets. One shows me exactly what the 'little one' looks like now, inside my womb. Another tells me in dubious language exactly how abortions are performed. The last, entitled 'A Woman's Right To Choose', tells me how 'abortion violates women'.

Since there are casualties on both sides in any conflict, I wanted to see what it was like on the other side of the fence, at the abortion clinic; but there was the obstacle of the compulsory pregnancy test. So this story belongs to Sam, who recently went to an abortion clinic a short walk and a whole world away from the Life advice centre.

'The first thing you do is give a urine sample to confirm that you actually are pregnant,' she says. 'Then you go into a little room with a counsellor and they tell you: "This is just a formality which we have to follow by law.

We can confirm that you are pregnant – is there definitely no way that you can have this baby?" You say no and then the doctor examines you, they tell you how the operation will be performed and you pick the nearest clinic to you.

'There is no mention of adoption or how you might manage should you decide to keep the child. That suited me because my mind was made up – but what about people who aren't entirely sure? It's not counselling – more a set speech that's quickly over. It was as if by admitting that abortion wasn't an everyday experience for most women the clinic's whole philosophy would be shattered. Is there nobody that's neutral that you can go and see?'

Franca Tranza at Marie Stopes, which runs several abortion clinics, says: 'As far as the individual woman is concerned, it doesn't matter what the different pressure groups are saying.

'This week you couldn't get away from abortion on the news, but these are real women with real-life dilemmas. Women come in all the time saying they've always been pro-life or pro-choice but now it's happening to them it's different.' Ironically, it seems the targets of the abortion propaganda war, pregnant and vulnerable women, are the ones left out in the cold while the pressure groups fight on.

A carefree abortion can be embarrassing

By Decca Aitkenhead

Pregnancy counsellors are much like agony aunts; most women in search of their services will opt for the one they think will give them what they're looking for. A young, pregnant, frightened Ann Widdecombe would be a surprising arrival at the doors of a Marie Stopes clinic, and I would be unlikely to take my troubles to the Society for the Protection of Unborn Children. So each side invests heavily in scare stories about the enemy ('They keep the remains in the sink, you know!'; 'Nuns show girls a bucket!' etc.), with very little to go on. This seems a mistake, so, one morning this week, I invented a calamitous pregnancy, and took myself off for some pro-life counselling.

SPUC and Life each have little houses in central London, located, rather unfortunately, on backstreets. At Life, a woman who looks like a kindly country granny listens calmly as I describe a standard plight: unwanted pregnancy, horror at the prospect of inadequate, impoverished parenthood, and endless sound reasons why this baby is plainly an appalling idea.

'Do you know what your baby looks like?' she smiles. She gets out some pictures to show me. 'Eight weeks now, did you say?' she coaxes, 'or was it nine?' She is keen to upgrade my foetus to the caption which says it can now curl its fingers round an object. She addresses all her comments to my stomach, and they are punctuated – I'm sorry, but there's no other way to describe them – with pregnant pauses.

'What do you think your baby would say to his mummy,' she wonders, 'if he could talk to you? I think he'd ask, "Are you going to let me live?"' If my answer's no, I will certainly go to hell. But that will be the least of my problems. I'll be sending myself to 'living hell' first.

It is always pleasing to discover that your adversaries are every bit as objectionable as you had suspected. Pro-life's trump card is vicious: abortion is devastating, and you can never escape the scars of guilt and shame. Thank God, then, for pro-choice liberals. Only we heard a lot from them this week, and their view seemed to be – stop me if you've heard this one before – that abortion is devastating, and you can never escape the . . .

In their anxiety to show that they do not take abortion lightly, defenders of the Abortion Act have ended up sounding like their opponents. On Radio 4's *Call Nick Ross* last Tuesday, pro-choicers were falling over each other to talk up the trauma. 'No woman ever takes the decision to abort lightly,' they chanted, and there is 'always a terrible emotional price to pay'.

One of the unexpected benefits of having had an abortion is that I find myself able to say with confidence that they are wrong. To be pregnant at university at 20 was a desperate misfortune, but to have the baby was quite literally unthinkable. So it was no harder to 'decide' to abort than it would have been to 'decide' to have a limb amputated after a horrible car crash. These are clearly decisions one would never want to make – but nor, in such circumstances, can they meaningfully be called 'decisions' at all.

In that sense, let us be candid: the decision to have an abortion is indeed sometimes taken 'lightly'.

'Society today denies women who have had abortions the "permission" to grieve,' according to the founder of British Victims of Abortion. The opposite is in fact true. It is no longer taboo to have had an abortion, but absolutely taboo to say, 'I had an abortion, and actually wasn't traumatised at all.' I searched myself for doubt, trauma, guilt, and found none, nor has any surfaced since. The women leaving the clinic that afternoon were a model of relieved and happy womanhood.

This account of abortion is one you will often hear in private, but rarely in public. It is certainly not universal, nor necessarily even the norm, but it does disprove the notion that abortion is, by definition, a monstrous ordeal. Pro-lifers dismiss this experience as denial, or delayed reaction, but as they are fighting a crude crusade, such spurious stabs are no more than their right. It is the vaguely liberal pro-choicers' refusal to accommodate this account which is unacceptable. Nick Ross gave a perfect, if unwitting, illustration of this in his introduction last Tuesday. 'If you had an abortion, was it merely a modern convenience to bail you out of trouble? Or,' and here his tone fell, 'was it a private tragedy that haunts you still?' The carefree abortion is frowned upon in polite pro-choice circles, largely because it gets tangled in with anxiety about a flippant, take-it-or-leave-it approach to the whole weighty business of parenting. In fact, it signifies the exact opposite. It is women who treat motherhood with proper respect who are able to terminate an unwanted and plainly ill-advised pregnancy with so little doubt, and who therefore feel little trauma or later regret. They do not imagine they have made a glib or trivial choice, but an important and sensible one.

It is no longer taboo to have had an abortion, but absolutely taboo to say, 'I had an abortion, and actually wasn't traumatised at all.'

Women who decline to feign devastation also cause alarm within the pro-choice lobby because they are seen as a PR liability. Pro-lifers will be thrilled to scandalise about those girls going round saying they had an abortion at the drop of a hat and didn't give two hoots, confirming all those age-old accusations of abortion campaigners as callous baby-haters.

But in their concern to throw off that charge, pro-choicers have succeeded in doing women a damaging disservice.

SPUC sent me away with an ominous book all about post-abortion trauma – collected works of anguish, the main symptoms of which, apparently, are guilt and shame. It is hard to imagine what pro-life post-abortion counsellors can possibly say to make women feel better, what with all the living hell and the eternal hell to look forward to. But when abortion's very defenders are also insisting all women must feel awful, it is hardly surprising that so many do. The ones who still manage not to feel guilty then feel guilty and anxious about their 'unnatural' absence of guilt.

Reading the book, a sad irony becomes clear. Those women shattered by their experience of abortion are those who terminated a pregnancy which they desperately wanted to continue, but, for various agonising reasons, felt unable to. Self-recrimination, resentment and regret all, understandably, follow. It is women who categorically do not want to keep their babies who suffer least; and yet it is these women the pro-choice movement finds most embarrassing.

Supporters of the abortion law have enjoyed so little serious challenge that their logic has grown flabby. It was pitifully easy for Cardinal Winning to wrong-foot them this week – a simple offer of money had campaigners huffing and puffing about 'bribes' and 'buying babies', because they have allowed themselves to be drawn into a version of abortion where there are acceptable candidates (poor mothers, rape victims and so on) and unacceptable ones, women who simply do not want to have a baby, otherwise known as selfish teenage strumpets.

The movement should have been strong enough to turn around to the good Cardinal, smile broadly, and say, fine, you can offer all the money you like – it makes not a whit of difference.

Pro-lifers attack leap in 'social' abortion

Nine out of ten terminations purely for mother's sake, figures show

By Steve Doughty

Anti-abortion campaigners claim new figures show nine out of ten terminations are carried out on 'social' grounds.

Statistics published yesterday also reveal that one in five conceptions by women in England and Wales ends in abortion, compared with fewer than one in ten in 1970.

The proportion of operations performed to protect the 'mental health' of the woman – grounds condemned by opponents as tantamount to abortion on demand – has climbed steeply in the 1990s.

The first detailed analysis of abortion trends published by Government statisticians in six years also shows how an increasing proportion of terminations is carried out in the first nine weeks of pregnancy.

Anti-abortion campaigners yesterday claimed this showed women were being rushed into terminations without the time for counselling. Increasingly accurate detectors are, however, enabling women to discover they are pregnant much earlier.

The figures come at a time of acute sensitivity over the issue, with the Pro-Life Alliance fielding more than 50 election candidates against pro-abortion MPs.

The leader of Scotland's Roman Catholics, Cardinal Thomas Winning, also sparked controversy by offering financial support to pregnant women who choose to keep their babies.

According to the analysis in *Population Trends*, the journal of the Office for National Statistics, the proportion of abortions carried out because of risk to the mother's mental or physical health rose from 83 per cent in 1991 to 89 per cent in 1995. In women under 20 the figure is 95 per cent.

More than 150,000 abortions are carried out in England and Wales each year.

Figures show that 42 per cent were carried out earlier than nine weeks into the pregnancy during 1995, compared with 36 per cent in 1990.

More than one in four children will see their parents divorce by the time they are 16, Government analysts warned yesterday.

Office for National Statistics expert John Haskey said that divorce jeopardised children's successful development and adjustment into adulthood.

Under-16s have more than 4,000 abortions

By David Fletcher, Health Correspondent

The number of girls who become pregnant has risen for the first time in four years, a report disclosed yesterday.

A total of 7,800 girls under 16 became pregnant in 1994, according to the Office for National Statistics. Just over half the pregnancies – 4,100 – were ended by abortion.

The rate of girl pregnancies was 8.3 in every 1,000, compared with 8.1 the previous year. The peak was 10.1 in 1990.

Only 54 per cent of conceptions occurred within marriage in 1994, compared with 56 per cent the previous year.

The vast majority – 92 per cent – of the 85,000 teenagers who became pregnant in 1994 were unmarried and 35 per cent of them had an abortion. Overall, 802,000 women became pregnant in England and Wales, a decrease of 17,000 – two per cent – over 1993.

A quarter of married women who became pregnant had an abortion, compared with nearly four out of five unmarried women.

Overall, almost one in five conceptions was aborted. The abortion rate of 35 per cent among teenagers dropped steadily to only 13 per cent among those aged 30-34.

The rate rose as women got older to more than 20 per cent among those aged 35-39, and to 40 per cent – the highest rate for any age group – among those aged 40 and over.

The report highlights major regional differences. Pregnancy rates were highest in east London and lowest in Cambridge. Abortion rates were highest in Kensington, Chelsea and Westminster and lowest in Suffolk and north-west Anglia.

Barnsley, Doncaster and south-east London had the highest pregnancy rates for girls under 16, while Cambridge and Barnet had the lowest.

The abortion debate

A document published last week which suggested that a foetus can feel pain has stirred up the abortion debate once again. Here, two women argue for and against

'It is up to those who would deny unborn infants protection to prove to us that they cannot feel pain'

One of the problems facing society on the question of foetal sentience is that, in the present state of science, it is impossible directly to assess, observe or prove with absolute certainty that pain is being experienced in another subject.

Our knowledge of pain rests on personal experience. We can also deduce a great deal from the development of the central nervous system and from the physical reactions to stimuli (which begin in the human foetus at around six weeks' gestation).

The whole crux of the issue was recently summed up by Professor Christopher Hull (Vice President of the Royal College of Anaesthetists) when he said: 'So far as I am concerned, I would be prepared to accept that foetuses do not feel pain when somebody proves to me that they don't feel pain. But until that time, I would have to assume that they do.'

As a professor of anaesthetics, Christopher Hull must be well versed in the arguments used to deny foetal sentience – that 'pain is a function of consciousness'; that 'one must be aware and able to remember'. But when Radio Four's *World At One* questioned him, he said: 'We don't know.' As the balance of evidence shows that, by the 10th week of life, a foetus has present and functional the anatomical structures necessary for the experience of pain, it is up to those who would deny unborn infants protection to prove to us that they cannot feel pain.

And, so far, all their claims are based on supposition, including the contention that awareness and sentience are solely functions of the upper part of the brain – the cerebral cortex. Growing evidence shows that the thalamus (the lower part of the brain which develops early in gestation) probably plays a more crucial role in consciousness and awareness than was previously recognised.

Much of this information has come from studies of babies with anencephaly (an abnormality where the cerebral cortex fails to develop). A group of clinicians from the University of California, reporting on such a study, stated: 'It neither logically nor physiologically follows that anencephalic infants by definition can neither feel nor experience pain.' To ignore actual pain reaction on the basis that a cerebral cortex was required amounts to 'begging the question of where pain [is] experienced.'

Since 1941, we have known that the foetus first reacts at only five or six weeks' gestation when touched about the mouth. These reactions extend until around the 12th week of life, when the child has almost the complete range of cutaneous responses – that is, no matter where touched, it will react.

The argument that this relates simply to reflex responses will stand up to examination only if we know for certain that the nerves responsible for reflex action develop before those of the pain pathways. Evidence suggests the reverse to be the case. In other words, there is a distinct possibility that the foetus may feel pain before it has reflex movements.

My opposition to abortion has always been based on the humanity of the foetus about which we, as a society, show so little care. The codes of practice governing animal experimentation in most parts of the western world require those involved to establish that any sentient creature they use is not subject to needless pain. In Australia, they must also 'assume that foetuses have the same requirements for anaesthesia as adult animals of the same species'. It is alarming that in Britain we are nowhere near such a consideration for the unborn of our own species.

Elizabeth Peacock
Joint Secretary of the All-Party
Parliamentary Pro-Life Group

My opposition to abortion has always been based on the humanity of the foetus about which we, as a society, show so little care

'Doctors do not wish to inflict suffering on foetuses, but to relieve the suffering of women'

The All-Party Parliamentary Pro-Life Group's report which claims that foetuses may feel pain from the 10th week of development is the latest in a number of attempts by those who oppose abortion to claim that foetuses suffer.

'Foetal pain' is an issue with an agenda. Despite the claims of the Pro-Life group, there is no 'new science' to show that foetuses suffer pain during abortion. In fact, the weight of evidence is rather that they are incapable of suffering – at least in the earlier stages of pregnancy during which the overwhelming majority of abortions occurs.

No one can doubt that foetuses, from early on in their development, respond to physical stimuli. Experts know that when blood samples are taken from a foetus in late gestation, the procedure causes a rise in stress hormones associated with pain. But writing in *The Lancet*, the authors of a recent paper discussing this phenomenon were careful to stress that 'a hormonal response cannot be equated with the perception of pain'. When, at the request of the Department of Health, Professor Maria Fitzgerald reviewed current scientific knowledge on foetal pain, she confirmed that the development of the brain and the nervous system ruled out foetal perceptions of pain, at least prior to 26 weeks' gestation. True pain experience, she suggested, could develop only 'postnatally, along with memory, anxiety and other brain functions'.

Fitzgerald is Professor of Neurobiology in the Department of Anatomy and Developmental Biology at University College, London, so you'd have thought her paper would have resolved it. But no. Those who wish to make a case that the foetus does feel pain, in particular during abortion, scrabbled to find counter argument. And so the discussion goes on.

It's worth asking: why has it become such an issue? Members of the Pro-Life Group are opposed to all abortions, whether or not they cause pain to the foetus. Even if it could be demonstrated beyond all doubt that foetuses don't feel pain, they would still object to abortion. For them, the issue is that abortion is wrong, however and whenever it's done. They are against it in principle. So why not oppose it in principle? Why focus on such an esoteric issue as foetal pain?

Increasingly, the anti-choice movement tries to shift public discussion from why women end pregnancies to how they are ended. Those who oppose abortion stress the consequence of the procedure for the foetus, never the consequence of the pregnancy for the woman. The anti-choice lobby knows that most women are touched by images of baby-like foetuses floating serenely in amniotic fluid and spelling out in graphic detail how an abortion is performed is far more likely to win them support than a graphic description of the reasons why a woman feels she needs to end her pregnancy.

The discussion of foetal pain has the same effect. The thought of a suffering foetus is repugnant even to a woman who wants an abortion. But doctors are not sadists. They do not perform abortions because they wish to inflict suffering on foetuses, but because they want to relieve the suffering of women.

By raising the issue of foetal pain, those who oppose abortion in principle are trying to reset its agenda. They turn attention to the possible suffering of foetuses to shift attention from the actual suffering of women seeking abortion. In the abstract debate about foetal pain, it's important that the undeniable, manifest pain of women is never forgotten.

Ann Furedi, Director of the Birth Control Trust

Change in Hippocratic oath to back abortion

An updated version of medicine's Hippocratic oath ran into trouble last night for the backing it gave to abortion and the lower priority given to prolonging human life.

The British Medical Association has drawn up a draft replacement for the historic code which established the founding principles of medical practice in the fifth century BC. But opponents of abortion and anti-euthanasia campaigners hit out at the new wording.

The original oath, drawn up by the Greek physician Hippocrates, includes pledges to 'give no deadly medicine to anyone if asked' and 'not give to a woman a pessary to produce abortion'.

The new version, which is designed to reflect the reality of medical practice in the late twentieth century, substitutes a different form of thinking.

It proposes that doctors throughout the world should swear: 'I recognise the special value of human life but also know that the prolongation of human life is not the only aim of health care. Where abortion is permitted, I agree that it should take place only within an ethical and legal framework.' But Paul Tully, of the Society for the Protection of Unborn Children, said: 'It is really an insult to the Hippocratic tradition that they have taken it upon themselves to rewrite the oath in this way. It is plain that Hippocrates and his followers took the view that abortion was unethical.

'Changing the oath is not going to make it ethical. It is a lot of whitewash, a lot of nonsense.' Dr Peggy Norris, who chairs the anti-euthanasia organisation, Alert, preferred the clear wording of the original which committed doctors to giving 'no deadly medicine. I think this new wording could be misinterpreted and could give doctors more leeway.' The BMA said it decided to produce an updated version to bring the ethical code into line with modern practice.

The draft emphasises doctors' duty to make patients their 'first concern'. The BMA chairman, Dr Sandy Macara, said: 'It is as important as ever it was for doctors to have an agreed statement of ethical principles.' The BMA, which has campaigned for five years to update the oath, gathered examples of ethical codes from all over the world to produce the draft document.

Man Alive

Men unheard in abortion debate

By Joe Armstrong

It's very difficult to know what men's attitudes to abortion are. Little scientific study has been done. A detailed summary of scientific research relating to the psychological and social aspects of abortion produced by the Psychological Society of Ireland makes not a single mention of the effects of abortion on men. As one academic put it: 'People haven't asked men for their views.'

An *Irish Times*/MRBI poll of November 1992 found that as many as 73 per cent of men (and 72 per cent of women) were in favour of abortion in certain circumstances. Some 20 per cent of men (and 18 per cent of women) were in favour of abortion for anybody who wanted it.

Thirty-five per cent of men (compared to 30 per cent of women) favoured abortion if there was a threat to the physical life of the mother, while a further 18 per cent of men (and 24 per cent of women) approved of abortion if there was a threat to the woman's life or a danger of her committing suicide.

Only 17 per cent of men opposed abortion in any circumstances, compared to 23 per cent of women.

The polarised debate between pro-life and pro-choice positions in this country in recent years makes it next to impossible for the 70,000 to 80,000 Irish women – and remember that may be a conservative estimate – who have had abortions to contribute their experience to the public debate.

Similarly, the tens of thousands of Irish men whose progeny were aborted remain silent. Last Monday, Father Padraig McCarthy, writing in the letters page of this newspaper, seemed to suggest that he was sad that most women who have abortions experience more positive responses, such as relief, rather than such negative responses as guilt.

Such views are not conducive to some 150,000 Irish men and women to contribute the truth as they see it from the valid perspective of their own experience. All the Irish women interviewed by author Ruth Fletcher for one recent study considered they had made the right decision in having an abortion.

Some 20 per cent of men (and 18 per cent of women) were in favour of abortion for anybody who wanted it

Women fear that if they admit to positive or negative feelings after an abortion their experiences will be hijacked and remoulded by one or the other lobby as proof that its own strongly held position on abortion is the right one. A woman's expression of regret after an abortion can be reconstructed by the pro-life movement as remorse, while the same woman's value for foetal life as more than an inconsequential bunch of cells can be disparaged by the pro-choice movement. Both lobbies can fail to recognise the complexity of the woman's decision and ignore the piebald truth that lies in that space between black and white.

Men can be very threatened by women's power to abort, says Domhnall Casey, a Dublin-based psychologist and psychotherapist. 'Men don't have a say in it. It shows the power of women. Women can kill you at a swipe.' Domhnall Casey believes that men can be affronted at a subconscious level by the power their mother once had over them in the womb. In evolutionary terms it appears that women, not men, were in the dominant position. Mother and earth are fruitful, while men just exist. The words maternal and material have the same Greek root connected in mythology to woman as earth goddess.

The words geography and

geology share the root Gaia or Ge, the name of the primeval earth goddess – the first creature, a female born from Chaos. As such, the creation story in Genesis which suggests that Adam arrived first can be seen as a usurpation.

Against this backdrop, men's concern to control women's reproductive capacity can be seen as a typical male defensive posture and an attempt to control the more powerful female.

Domhnall Casey says: 'Abortion shows women's power to emasculate men. The woman has complete control.' Up to the last 20 years, he says, society reinforced the isolation of men.

'Now, because of the prevailing ethos and consciousness-raising, men are trying to be more connected to women and children. Parental duties and roles are increasingly being shared. Men, more and more, feel connected to the foetus. They are connected in sympathy but not physically – they can't be.

'When the question of abortion arises, these men are frustrated, alienated, faced with their limitations and with the power of women. Before, women rebelled against men who tried to force their will on them. Now the problem is to accommodate the caring will of men who wish to be involved.'

Ailbhe Smyth, director of the Women's Education, Research and Resource Centre at University College Dublin (UCD), says: 'Abortion as an experience is primarily that of a woman, psychologically and physically. It's not unimportant for the man, but it's not a primary experience. Up to the last 20 to 25 years we didn't know about that experience for women. We haven't yet started seeing how men relate to that.' Dr Sheila Jones, medical director of the Irish Family Planning Association, says it is good if both partners are counselled about an abortion. 'While the decision is the woman's, the more involvement of the male the better.' Dr Jones says quite a number of men accompany their partners to England, but often the woman does not want the man to be involved, especially if the relationship is over.

Dr Geraldine Moane of the Department of Psychology at UCD says that sometimes women have abortions because they do not consider the man they are involved with is a suitable partner (an explanation which could further explain why men keep quiet about an abortion): 'Some men have been angry at being excluded from the decision. Others have forced the pace. Others seem happy to leave it to the woman; [men's] involvement in the process influences their responses.'

Debbie Morrissey has counselled men and women in England about abortion. She says men often have a bad initial reaction to hearing a woman with whom they are involved is pregnant. They can also feel bad about the abortion – especially if they have been anti-abortion.

Frequently, they do not understand the complexity of the woman's dilemma: 'I don't want to have an abortion but I don't want this baby'.

Ms Morrissey worked for almost a decade with the Marie Stopes organisation in Britain in the past. She says that men often fail to understand that a woman can be upset after an abortion. Men who accompany their partners can also be embarrassed to come into a clinic, she says. 'They think it'll be full of stern women, making them guilty.' Some men, she says, are really awful. They've dragged their partners along. A man's reaction can depend on what type of relationship the couple has. 'It's frustrating for men, because it's the woman's choice. The woman has a lot of power. He has zilch, absolutely no power. Quite often women can feel quite empowered.' Debbie Morrissey does not believe depression in either a man or a woman is caused by the abortion. 'It's how they feel about themselves; or if they had poor mothering or fathering,' she says of women. 'That's also true for men. Like anything significant, it can bump up stuff from your childhood.'

'When the question of abortion arises, these men are frustrated, alienated, faced with their limitations and with the power of women'

If men got pregnant would they really allow the State to act like Big Brother vis-a-vis reproductive choices they might or might not want to make about their unborn child, wanted or unwanted? Not for the first time this whole area makes one feel that were men able to conceive and bear children, society might be structured in a vastly different way.

• The above is an extract from the *Man Alive* men's health column in *The Irish Times* by columnist Joe Armstrong.

INDEX

ADDITIONAL RESOURCES

Abortion Law Reform Association (ALRA)
Education for Choice
11-13 Charlotte Street
London, W1P 1HD
Tel: 0171 637 7264
The Abortion Law Reform Association is a national pressure group which has been working since 1936 to enshrine in law and in practice a women's right to safe, free and legal abortion based upon her own informed choice.

Birth Control Trust (BCT)
16 Mortimer Street
London, W1N 7RD
Tel: 0171 580 9360
Fax: 0171 637 1378
Publishes a wide range of books, pamphlets and reports on reproductive health including issues such as abortion, teenage pregnancy and sterilisation. An SAE is required if seeking their publication list.

British Humanist Association
47 Theobald's Road
London, WC1X 8SP
Tel: 0171 430 0908
Fax: 0171 430 1271
Publishes a wide range of free briefings including the issues of abortion, euthanasia and surrogacy.

British Pregnancy Advice Service (BPAS)
Austy Manor
Wootton Wawen
Solihull
West Midlands, B95 6BX
Tel: 01564 793225
Fax: 01564 794935
Helps and advises women faced with an unwanted pregnancy.

Brook Advisory Centres
165 Gray's Inn Road
London, WC1X 8UD
Tel: 0171 713 9000
Fax: 0171 833 8182
Provides free and confidential advice for young people up to the age of 25 on sex and contraception.

Christian Medical Fellowship (CMF)
157 Waterloo Road
London, SE1 8XN
Tel: 0171 928 4694
Fax: 0171 620 2453
A network of approximately 4,500 doctors and 600 medical students throughout the UK and Republic of Ireland. They produce a range of booklets and leaflets.

Family and Youth Concern
322 Woodstock Road
Oxford, OX2 7NS
Tel: 01865 556848
Fax: 01865 552774
A national organisation with no political or religious affiliations. They produce leaflets, pamphlets, books, reports and video tapes on matters affecting the family.

Family Planning Association
2-12 Pentonville Road
London, N1 9FP
Tel: 0171 837 5432
Fax: 0171 837 3042
Provides information on all aspects of family planning including termination. Their helpline, 0171 837 4044 Mon-Fri 9am-7pm, is run jointly with the Health Education Authority and is answered by qualified healthcare workers.

LIFE
LIFE House
Newbold Terrace
Leamington Spa
Warwickshire, CV32 4EA
Tel: 01926 421587
Fax: 01926 336497
Educates people about the nature of abortion and its consequences; to help women, to prevent abortion by offering free pregnancy counselling and to help any pregnant women.

Marie Stopes International
153-157 Cleveland Street
London, W1P 5PG
Tel: 0171 574 7400
Fax: 0171 574 7417
Provides reproductive healthcare/ family planning services and information, to enable individuals all over the world to have children by choice, not by chance.

National Abortion Campaign
The Print House
18 Ashwin Street
London, E8 3DL
Tel: 0171 923 4976
Fax: 0171 923 4979
Works to secure the right for women to make their own decision about abortion. Produces publications.

Society for the Protection of the Unborn Child (SPUC)
Phyllis Bowman House
5/6 St Matthew Street
Westminster
London, SW1P 2JT
Tel: 0171 222 5845
Fax: 0171 222 0603
SPUC defends and promotes the human right to life from conception onwards.

Support after Termination for Abnormality (SAFTA)
73 -75 Charlotte Street
London, W1P 1LB
Tel: 0171 631 0280 (admin)
0171 631 0285 (helpline)
Gives support to parents when an abnormality is detected in their baby. Please note that SAFTA must have a stamped, addressed envelope for student project inquiries. They have recently published: *Help for fathers*, *Help for grandparents*, *Talking to children* and *The next pregnancy*. Available for £1 per copy.

Women's Health
52 Featherstone Street
London, EC1Y 8RT
Tel: 0171 251 6333
Fax: 0171 608 0928
Provides a variety of leaflets on many aspects of women's health including advice on abortions. Ask for their publications list and order form.

ACKNOWLEDGEMENTS

The publisher is grateful for permission to reproduce the following material.

While every care has been taken to trace and acknowledge copyright, the publisher tenders its apology for any accidental infringement or where copyright has proved untraceable. The publisher would be pleased to come to a suitable arrangement in any such case with the rightful owner.

Chapter One: An overview

Abortion key facts, © Marie Stopes International, *Abortion law*, © British Pregnancy Advisory Service (BPAS), © *The arguments for and against abortion*, © British Pregnancy Advisory Service (BPAS), *Abortion*, © Brook Advisory Centre, 1996, *Legal abortions*, © Office for National Statistics, *A matter of life or death*, © Telegraph Group Limited, London 1997, *Religious views on abortion*, © National Abortion Campaign, July 1991, *Abortion statistics*, © Brook Advisory Centres, 1997.

Chapter Two: The moral dilemma

The campaign for choice, © ALRA, *Abortion*, © British Humanist Association, *Growing support for abortion*, © The Scotsman, February 1997, *Abortion – the key issue*, © Christian Medical Fellowship, *Would you take your daughter to the abortion clinic?*, © The Sunday Mirror, April 1997, *Three reasons why abortion is not the answer*, © The Daily Record, February 1997, *Nobel winner backs abortion 'for any reason'*, © The Independent, February 1997, *Unwanted pregnancy and abortion*, © ALRA, *A woman's right to choose?*, © LIFE, *Hard questions answered*, © LIFE, *Abortion care*, © Woman's Health, May 1996, *Abortion*, © Family Planning Association, *Legal abortions – by marital status*, © Office for National Statistics, *Crying shame of the past*, © The Guardian, March 1997, *A campaign to abort*, © The Economist, January 1997, *The abortion debate*, © Telegraph Group Limited, London 1997, *The abortion lifeline*, © The Daily Mail, March 1997, *A little money won't change their minds*, © The Daily Record, March 1997, *Catholics back pro-choice abortion stance*, © Press Association, February 1997, *Abortion*, © The Independent on Sunday, March 1997, *A carefree abortion can be embarrassing*, © The Guardian, March 1997, *Pro-lifers attack leap in 'social' abortion*, © The Daily Mail, March 1997, *Under 16s have more than 4,000 abortions*, © Telegraph Group Limited, London 1996, *The abortion debate*, © The Guardian, July 1996, *Change in Hippocratic oath to back abortion*, © The Scotsman, March 1997, *Man Alive*, © Joe Armstrong, February 1997.

Photographs and Illustrations

Pages 1, 30: Andrew Smith, pages 6, 15, 28: Michaela Bloomfield, page 17: ALRA.

Craig Donnellan
Cambridge
September, 1997